DO-IT-YOURSELF

Painting

FOR

DUMMIES®

by Katharine Kaye McMillan, PhD,
and Patricia Hart McMillan

Wiley Publishing, Inc.

Painting Do-It-Yourself For Dummies®

Published by
Wiley Publishing, Inc.
111 River St.
Hoboken, NJ 07030-5774
www.wiley.com

WILEY

About the Authors

Katharine Kaye McMillan, PhD, is a social cognitive psychologist who writes do-it-yourself decorating advice in her online *Design Doctor* column. She is the coauthor with her mother and mentor, Patricia Hart McMillan, of *Home Decorating For Dummies,* 2nd Edition, *Glass Tile: Inspirations for Kitchens and Baths, Sun Country Style,* and *House Comfortable. Where the Pros Live,* her weekly feature series on how trendsetters and tastemakers really design for themselves, runs weekly in the *Palm Beach Post*'s "Florida Home" section. She is a contributing writer to *Florida Design,* the leading internationally distributed decorating magazine. An expert in masculinity and self-concept, she teaches psychology at private and public colleges in South Florida. She appears on national and regional television shows, talk radio, and trades her do-it-yourself design secrets at home shows nationwide with Patricia Hart McMillan.

Patricia Hart McMillan was Interior Design Editor of *1,001 Decorating Ideas* (later *Home*), one of the first dedicated do-it-yourself magazines with a multimillion reader circulation in the U.S., Canada, and Japan. She became Remodeling Editor of *Home Mechanix Magazine,* whose do-it-yourself readers included semi-professional and professional carpenters, painters, paper-hangers, floor-installers, and plumbers. On at least one occasion, she hung wallcovering for publication! As Editor in Chief of *20/20 Magazine,* she helped launch a retail shop design series entitled *Blueprint for Success,* which continues. Private decorating clients include some "household names" as well as newlyweds with big dreams and small budgets. She's author and coauthor of eight books and at work on four more dealing with interior design, contemporary architecture, architectural glass tile, and historic houses and gardens. Her trendspotting articles and profiles of nationally known designers appear in newspapers, magazines, and online.

Publisher's Acknowledgments

We're proud of this book; please send us your comments through our Dummies online registration form located at www.dummies.com/register/.

Some of the people who helped bring this book to market include the following:

Contributors: Judy Tremore, Traci Cumbay, Brenda Brink, Kevin Funkhouser, Jamie Funkhouser, Jenny Zahm, Luke Funkhouser

Acquisitions, Editorial, and Media Development

Senior Project Editor: Alissa Schwipps

Acquisitions Editor: Tracy Boggier

Copy Editor: Sarah Faulkner

Editorial Program Coordinator: Erin Calligan Mooney

Senior Editorial Manager: Jennifer Ehrlich

Editorial Assistants: Joe Niesen, Leeann Harney, David Lutton

Cover Photos: Matt Bowen

Cartoons: Rich Tennant (www.the5thwave.com)

Composition Services

Senior Project Coordinator: Kristie Rees

Layout and Graphics: Shelley Norris, Kathie Rickard

Photography: Matt Bowen

Anniversary Logo Design: Richard Pacifico

Proofreaders: Jessica Kramer, Linda Quigley

Indexer: Potomac Indexing, LLC

Special Help
Elizabeth Rea, Tracy Barr

Publishing and Editorial for Consumer Dummies

Diane Graves Steele, Vice President and Publisher, Consumer Dummies

Joyce Pepple, Acquisitions Director, Consumer Dummies

Kristin A. Cocks, Product Development Director, Consumer Dummies

Michael Spring, Vice President and Publisher, Travel

Kelly Regan, Editorial Director, Travel

Publishing for Technology Dummies

Andy Cummings, Vice President and Publisher, Dummies Technology/General User

Composition Services

Gerry Fahey, Vice President of Production Services

Debbie Stailey, Director of Composition Service

Contents at a Glance

Table of Contents

Introduction

Do-it-yourselfers are a new breed of smart people who like to do it themselves. Picking up this book includes you in the breed and makes you one of those smart people. In this case, you're interested in doing your own painting. We already know that as a do-it-yourselfer, you're brainy, and you have a can-do attitude and a strong desire to save time, money, and energy doing it right the first time. We're here to help by offering you solid advice, showing you instructional photos, and cheering you on as you strive toward your goal.

This book gives you the best info in easy-to-get, can't-go-wrong bytes. We want you to get the best, professional-level outcome the very first time you take a roller to the wall. To that end, we give you all the basics from deciding what, when, and where to paint to finding out how to fix your projects when things go wrong. In no time at all, you'll be able to tackle any painting project in this book with efficiency, accuracy, and confidence.

About This Book

Painting Do-It-Yourself For Dummies is here to help you make your living space look like it received a makeover. Whether you're looking for a subtle makeover to enhance what you already have, or an extreme makeover to show the world a totally new look, you can find something to suit your style in this book. We show you how to prep your painting surface, and we give you the best in painting basics. Then we give you plenty of ideas for your walls, floors, and ceilings. A great color here, a little pattern there, and a whole lot of best practice painting techniques help create the ideal backdrop for your lifestyle.

This book breaks the projects down step by step and shows you the painting techniques that produce the best results. The stepwise approach is what sets this (do-it-yourself how-to) apart from the pack. Stepwise keeps your tasks on track.

You've heard the expression that a picture is worth a thousand words. To that end, we include more than 400 photographs and illustrations in this book. Seeing is believing — that sounds familiar, too — and it's also the quickest way to convey the most information. People learn well by observing, and we believe it's a better way than trial and error. If you want the positive reinforcement of living in a nicely painted room and not the punishment of smudges, drips, and ugly surfaces, read on!

We share the expert experience that we acquired while on the job in our own homes, in clients' homes, on movie sets, and in photography studios. We did the trial-and-error work so that you don't have to. In this book, we help you pick the right colors and the right tools for the job. We show you how to use the proper techniques so that you don't have to undo and redo. Your results, we can say with assurance, will meet and maybe even exceed your expectations.

Conventions Used in This Book

To make reading this book as easy as possible, we use the following conventions:

- ✔ We *italicize* new terms and provide a definition for them.
- ✔ We use `monofont` to identify all Web sites and e-mail addresses.
- ✔ We **bold** the keywords in bulleted lists.
- ✔ In Chapter 1, we introduce and describe all the tools you need for all the projects in this book. Flip to Chapter 1 whenever you need to know a tool's purpose, how to use it, or what it looks like, and for any cleaning or maintenance tips.
- ✔ We include extra tips and other interesting information in shaded sidebars throughout the chapters. This information is typically related to the step-by-step instructions for a nearby project.

Foolish Assumptions

We know what they say about making assumptions, but we made a few about you, the reader, before we started writing this book. We assume that you're a smart person who wants professional-level know-how without spending a whole lot of time, effort, and money to learn. Can you see yourself in one of the following groups?

- ✔ **First-time painters.** Never picked up a brush or roller in your life? Find out which brush or roller you need, how much time you'll have to spend, and what to expect from the painting process.

- ✔ **Timid painters.** Sure, you can paint any room a solid neutral color. But you're not so confident about painting bold colors or using faux finishing techniques. Glance at the photos in this book — is one of those exciting projects calling your name? We take the mystery out of using rags, sponges, colorwashes, glazes, and more, and you end up releasing your timidity and getting a fresh new look for your favorite rooms.

- ✔ **Do-it-yourselfers seeking better information.** You've painted. You've gotten less than stellar results. You realize that you just need to keep on painting. But, wait — you also realize that maybe you need a little more information about better techniques, top tools, and marvelous materials to make your next painting project outstanding.

If you fit into one of these groups — or if you'd like to fit into one of these groups — this book is for you! You're the do-it-yourselfer we had in mind as we painstakingly chose the projects for this book, wrote the text, took the photos, and put it all together. And now the finished product is in your hands just waiting to be read, broken in, and most likely spattered with paint.

How This Book Is Organized

We organize the chapters in *Painting Do-It-Yourself For Dummies* into four parts. Each part deals with a broad phase of painting, and each chapter targets specific information in detail.

Part I: Preparing for Your Painting Project

Always be prepared. Hey, that may not be the most original advice you've ever heard, but what does it take to be prepared? Here's the skinny on how to plan your design, pick paint, buy your brushes and supplies, and plan out your job. We walk you through taping, priming, and everything else you need to do to prepare your room. We show you how to make repairs so that you're painting on the best possible surface, and — if you're tired of drips and other mishaps — we give you a quick tour through the painting basics.

Part II: Painting Walls Like a Pro

Have you ever walked into a house, taken a look at the paint on the walls, and wondered, "How'd they do that?" If you're ready to move beyond a basic, solid paint color for your walls, this is the section for you. We show you how to use everyday items like rags, bags, and sponges to create a unique finish on your walls. If you're interested in stripes, stencils, or blocks of colors (in random or checkerboard patterns), we give you step-by-step instructions to liven up your living space. In no time, you'll be painting your walls like a pro.

Part III: Covering Other Areas of Your Home

When you master the art of painting your walls, you may be ready to focus your attention on other areas of your home. Check out our tips on painting your ceiling, improving the look of your wood floors, and sprucing up your trim.

Part IV: The Part of Tens

Want to know more? Ten things more to be exact? This part includes all those tips and pointers that can make a difference in your painting project. The Part of Tens gives you quick and easy advice on choosing great colors and making your project perfect.

Icons Used in This Book

As you read through the book, you'll see icons — little pictures in the margins — that alert you to important information. Whenever you see an icon, look and learn!

The Tip icon flags bits of time- and hassle-saving information.

This sign reminds you to take a mental note.

This emblem lets you know what and where the pitfalls are.

Where to Go from Here

If you're the kind of person who reads every book cover to cover, get started! If you're the kind of person who just wants to get to the good parts, feel free to peruse the projects that interest you. This book is designed to be a resource, almost like an encyclopedia or a dictionary. You can go straight to the part that's most relevant to you. You can flip to a topic that you want to know about. You can scan the table of contents to find a section, or go to the index to find out about one item. If you're not sure what tools you need to do the job, start with Chapter 1. If you need to brush up on painting basics, head to Chapter 4. And if you're looking for inspiration, check out any chapter in Parts II and III. No matter where you go, enjoy the painting process and the excellent results you're sure to get!

Part I

Preparing for Your Painting Project

The 5th Wave   By Rich Tennant

"I know we're just painting the interior rooms, but the instructions specifically said to cover everything you didn't want to get paint on."

In this part . . .

You're probably eager to get started on one of the painting projects shown in this book. You may even be tempted to skip over this part and focus solely on the fun stuff. Wait! Before you flip toward the later sections in this book, you need to go over the important points in this part. Trust us, putting a lovely coat of paint or a faux finish on an ill-prepared wall isn't what you want.

In this part, we give you the basic info on the tools you need to have on hand before you get started. We show you how to prep your room or surface before painting, and we walk you through those necessary repairs. Finally, we go over the painting basics — refer to them early and often for best painting project results.

Chapter 1

Gathering What You Need

You'll save time and energy if you assemble the essential tools for your paint project before you crack open a paint can. Nothing's worse than leaving a partially wet wall, for instance, to get a tool you forgot. That's especially true if you're using latex paint (formulated to dry quickly and often within an hour) because when you get back, you won't be able to blend your next brush strokes with the dry paint, and those transitions will be obvious when you finish the job. To ensure that you don't find yourself in that position, make a list of everything you need — tools, paint products, cleanup supplies, and so on — and gather it all before you begin.

This chapter makes the task easy by listing and describing tools for safety and for prepping and repairing your project. We also tell you what to think about when selecting sealer, primer, and paint, including information on basic painting tools, such as brushes, rollers, and roller covers, and specialized tools for decorative paint finishes. In addition, you can find items to help make cleanup much more simple.

Assembling a Painter's Toolbox

A carpenter wouldn't start a job without having a saw, hammer, level, and other tools on hand. Likewise, you can eliminate frustration and delays while you're working if you assemble the right stuff ahead of time. These sections list all the tools and supplies you'll need, whether your paint project is simple or complex. And while you're making that list in preparation for the shopping trip, think about what you already have at home or what you have access to — at your parents' and friends' houses, for example.

Consider which items will likely serve you time and time again, such as putty knives, levels, stud finders, paintbrushes, and rollers, to name a few. It makes sense to look for quality when you're buying those multi-use tools. Quality doesn't necessarily mean paying top dollar either. Home improvement stores stock quality tools and sell them at a range of moderate prices. Your best bet is to buy the best one that you can afford.

Tools for safety

When you're working on household projects, such as painting a room, the old maxim "Better safe than sorry" is a good rule to follow. Preventing an accident or avoiding a health hazard is easier than recovering from it. So resist the temptation not to purchase safety equipment just to save money. Some safety tools, such as a ladder and scaffolding, are a long-term investment. Buy the best equipment that you can afford because you'll be using these items over and over again. For your overall health, and especially if you have allergies or are sensitive to strong chemicals, you won't want to skimp on the low-cost items either. See the following list and Figure 1-1 for details about safety items:

- **5- or 6-foot stepladder:** For working on or near the ceiling
- **Breathing mask:** Blocks dust and fumes from getting into your lungs
- **Goggles:** Keep paint, chemicals, dust, and dirt out of your eyes
- **Kneepads:** Think 40 years down the line — your knees will thank you then
- **Latex gloves:** Prevent contact allergies and speed up the cleanup process — they also protect your nails
- **Long-sleeved, loose fitting shirt and jeans or slacks:** Keep chemicals and other irritants off your skin
- **Painter's cap:** Protects your hair
- **Scaffolding:** Not essential for an indoor project, such as painting a room, but nice to have, especially when you're painting vaulted ceilings or giving the walls a faux finish (see the nearby sidebar on scaffolding for more information)

Figure 1-1: These safety items are essential for a do-it-yourselfer.

Ladder safety

The best, sturdiest ladders will send you tumbling to the ground if you don't follow these basic safety precautions when you're using one:

✔ Never, ever lean out to the side or try to brush some paint on a spot you missed that's just out of reach.

✔ Don't climb up onto the top rung or step. The top rungs are meant for handholds, not feet.

✔ If the ladder feels unstable, have a buddy hold it steady for you.

✔ Never step on the drop-down shelf on stepladders; the shelf is designed for holding paint buckets and tools, not people.

Tools for prep and repairs

Improvising and doing your project with items you have around the house may be possible. But tools designed for the task make the job easier and more time efficient. You can find the items you need for prep and repair work at hardware stores, home improvement centers, and discount stores, mostly for a relatively low cost. You may want to consider borrowing or renting more expensive items, such as a wallboard saw and wallboard screw gun.

The following tools come in handy when you're ready to prep your room prior to painting:

✔ **Chemical stripper:** This product removes old, damaged paint.

✔ **Denatured alcohol:** Use this product to clean up oil-based paint.

✔ **Electronic level:** Use this level to help you find plumb lines when you're painting stripes on a wall or straightening pictures.

Scaffolding: Buy, rent, or make your own

When you're painting a ceiling or doing faux finishes, scaffolding is great. With a scaffold, you can move around much more easily because you don't have to climb up and down a ladder to move it a foot or two. You don't have to worry about falling off a step or constantly moving tools or paint supplies on and off the drop-down shelf. You can build scaffolding by placing a 12-inch wide plank on two sawhorses or stepladders (just be sure to allow enough overhang on each side as a precaution to keep the plank in place). Or you can buy a scaffold that has hinges and folds up on itself for easy storage. If you don't think you'll use the scaffold often enough to justify the expense, consider borrowing or renting one. Most hardware and home improvement stores have all kinds of rental equipment available for do-it-yourselfers working on home improvement projects.

- ✔ **Etching acid:** Use this acid to prep the surface of concrete floors for painting.

- ✔ **Large bucket:** Fill with water and detergent for scrubbing surfaces.

- ✔ **Laundry bleach:** Bleach removes mold and mildew spores from your walls before you paint.

- ✔ **Primer:** This is a good undercoat for paint.

- ✔ **Screwdriver:** As always, you need one for fastening screws.

- ✔ **Sealer:** Use this item when you want to keep damaged areas from bleeding through your paint finish.

- ✔ **Sponge:** When you're scrubbing surfaces, you'll need a sponge. You also use them to create several faux finishes.

- ✔ **Sponge mop:** Use this tool to clean floors before painting them.

- ✔ **TSP cleanser:** This heavy-duty cleanser cleans surfaces without leaving residue.

- ✔ **Utility knife:** This knife is also known as a razor knife. You can use it for cutting wallpaper, scoring walls, cleaning up ragged edges on drywall, and dozens of other tasks. As the blade dulls, simply replace it with another. Just keep the knife and blades where children won't find them — they're super sharp. (See Figure 1-2 for an example.)

- ✔ **Vacuum cleaner and brush attachment:** Try this tool for an easy way to remove dust and debris.

- ✔ **Wallpaper remover solution:** This solution loosens glue from the wallpaper backing and from the wall.

Figure 1-2: A utility knife and a masonry chisel.

Sometimes you need to repair your walls before you can prep and paint. In those instances, you may need the following tools:

- ✔ **Broad knife:** When you're patching plaster, try a broad knife. Unless you plan to patch walls and ceilings throughout your home, borrow a broad knife from a family member or a friend. If that's not possible, go ahead and buy one. They aren't expensive, even if they sit on a shelf for the next 50 years. (See Figure 1-3 for a picture of a broad knife.)

Figure 1-3: A small putty knife and a broad knife are good repair tools.

- ✔ **Drywall mud and tape:** Use these two items to seal seams between patches and the wall.

- ✔ **Electric mixer:** Not just for baking; use just one beater for mixing plaster when you're repairing small cracks and holes.

- ✔ **Masonry chisel:** This tool helps you repair cracks in plaster or take grout from between tiles. (Refer to Figure 1-2 to see an example.)

- ✔ **Patching compound:** Use this compound to fill in holes and dents.

- ✔ **Putty knife:** Use this knife to apply patching compounds. A small putty knife can be used for so many tasks — other than putty — that it should be a household staple. (Check out Figure 1-3 to see how this knife compares to a broad knife.)

- ✔ **Sandpaper/sanding block:** Whenever you use patching compounds to fill in holes or have imperfections or blemishes on an area, you have to make the surface smooth again before painting. Various grits of sandpaper will do the trick. A sanding block isn't necessary, but using one makes the job easier on your fingers and hands. One block will last forever. (See Figure 1-4 for a sanding block with sandpaper.)

Figure 1-4: Steel wool pads, sanding block with sandpaper, and a tack cloth.

✔ **Steel wool pads:** Like sandpaper, this tool also works to smooth a surface. Because steel wool has a variety of uses, such as cleaning a grill, keep a supply on hand. (Figure 1-4 shows you an example of steel wool pads.)

✔ **Tack cloth:** This tool wipes up dust without scattering it and removes other residue when you're done with a project. (Refer to Figure 1-4 for an example.)

✔ **Trim shellac or sealer:** Use these materials to keep wood stains from bleeding through new paint.

✔ **Wood filler:** This filler is handy for patching holes and imperfections.

Tools for basic painting

A brush is a brush, and a roller is a roller, right? Not quite. Paintbrushes come in various sizes and shapes, and with different handles. You also have to decide what kind of bristles you want and at what cost. *Roller cages* (the skeletal frame that includes the handle and "ribs" that rotate) and their covers come in several lengths. You have to select the length of the nap on covers and what it's made of. You find helpful information about selecting the right tool for your project on the packaging, and you can ask a salesperson for help. And check out the overviews of paintbrushes and rollers in this chapter.

You can choose the size of a brush and its shape, such as tapered or flat-bottomed, according to the job it's designed for. The smaller brushes, called trim or sash brushes, come in 1- to 3-inch widths. They're intended for use in small, tight spaces, and if the bristles are tapered, you can expect them to get into corners and grooves much more easily than a flat-bottomed brush of the same size. Likewise, wider brushes (called paint or wall brushes) come in 3- to 5-inch widths and are designed for painting large flat surfaces. As you increase the width of the brush, you compromise control and precision. Handles are made of wood or plastic and have different shapes. Get a handle that feels comfortable in your hand. If you're using latex paint, select a brush that has synthetic bristles. Listed here are some of your choices (see Figure 1-5 for examples):

✔ **1-inch angled sash brush:** Choose one with a stubby handle to paint edges and trim. They're also available with flat ends and longer handles.

✔ **2-inch angled sash brush:** This brush is used for cutting in corners and edges, and painting narrow window sashes and sills.

✔ **3-inch flat bristle sash brush:** We recommend the regular handle; use it for wide trim and sashes.

✔ **3-inch wall brush:** Use this one for floors, walls, and ceilings.

✔ **Small chip brush:** Use this brush to get paint into tight corners and spaces.

Figure 1-5: A 2-inch angled sash brush, a small chip brush, and a 3-inch flat sash brush.

Rollers are available in mini to 12-inch (and bigger) sizes. The mini (or trim) rollers are good for painting woodwork and other small areas. To work on walls and ceilings, choose a 9-inch roller; the larger sizes are heavier and will make you tire more quickly. A roller cage with plastic ribs holds up better than cardboard cages. Plastic can be cleaned, and it lasts longer than a cheaper version. As with bristles on a paintbrush, roller nap is made from natural or synthetic fibers. Nap is available in various lengths, so use the one recommended for the surface you're painting. In general, the longer the nap, the more paint it will hold. See Figure 1-6 to see some differences among rollers, and as a guideline, use

- ¼-**inch nap** for smooth or fine surfaces, such as new walls, ceilings, wood doors, and trim
- ⅜-**inch nap** for smooth to light-textured walls
- ½-**inch nap** for most walls and medium rough surfaces, such as textured plaster, and concrete
- ¾-**inch nap** for rough surfaces, such as textured walls and ceilings, textured plaster, and concrete

If you want a general-purpose roller cover, select a ⅜- or ½-inch nap.

Figure 1-6: Smooth, slightly nappy, and thick roller covers.

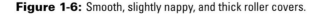

Selecting the best sealing and priming products

Sometimes sealing and priming isn't an either-or choice; your project may require both coats. People often use sealer and primer interchangeably, but they don't do the same job. Go to a paint specialist and explain what you want to do and any problems you have with the surface. Ask for advice and a low cost solution. In the meantime, here's the essential information about sealers, primers, and sealer/primer combinations.

Sealers keep stains, smoke, and soot on previously painted walls from bleeding through freshly applied paint. They seal the surface of soft and hard wood trim, hiding knot holes and stains. They also prevent textured ceilings from soaking up too much paint. Sealers are formulated for many different surfaces and to handle specific problems, so you have to find the right one. Prices vary depending on the formula. You may be able to opt for a combination sealer/primer, as we explain later in this sidebar.

It takes two coats of paint to make your walls look best. Use a primer as the first coat. Primers coat surfaces — walls, woodwork, trim, ceilings — so that the finish coats of paint adhere to the surfaces. They enhance the paint by providing a toothy surface that paint can stick to, helping to ensure even and smooth finish-coat coverage. Previously painted walls can act as a primer, but don't rely on the old paint if it's marred or if it's glossy paint and you want to use a latex eggshell or flat finish. On unpainted walls — plaster, Sheetrock (also called drywall), wood — the first coat soaks in and the second coat gives the wall the richness it deserves in the color you expect. You can do the wall twice in the finish coat, but that entails needless expense since finish paint costs more than primer. So use a primer for the first coat, and then paint over it with one coat of quality finish paint.

Even if you're working on a previously painted surface, you may need to prime, especially if bright or dark colors (think bright reds, black, and some shades of green) have been used. Primers can be tinted to provide a helpful color base if you're going over bright or dark colors. You can add mildewcides and moldicides to primers when you're painting high-moisture areas, such as bathrooms, kitchen backsplashes, laundry rooms, or even condo hallways in hurricane-prone areas.

When you go to the store to get your materials, let the salesperson know if you plan to do more than one thing — such as walls and woodwork — and ask whether a universal primer or combination sealer/primer would work best. Purchasing just one product reduces cost and eliminates the potential of storing several half-empty cans on a shelf. A combination sealer/primer may be more expensive than getting an inexpensive can of sealer and a cheap primer, but you'll save time.

The brush and roller are the most obvious tools you need for basic painting. But the following items are also helpful:

✔ **1-quart plastic paint bucket or container with lid:** Use one of these to mix and store paint. Smaller paint buckets or containers that have lids come in handy for storing leftover paint.

✔ **1- or 2-gallon household bucket:** Use these buckets to mix acid and water to etch concrete floors. If you're doing a faux finish, these buckets are great for mixing paint and glazes.

✔ **5-gallon bucket with a roller screen:** You can use this item for distributing paint on the cover rather than constantly refilling a flat roller tray.

✔ **5-in-1 tool:** This tool has a variety of uses. Use the blunt edge to open paint cans or as a flat-head screwdriver. The sharp edge is good for stripping or scraping paint. The pointed edge gets into grooves so that you can remove dirt, debris, or excess paint. With the back end, you can drive in nails or close paint cans. The curved side is handy for scraping off excess paint when you're cleaning the roller. And with the bonus "tear drop" in the center, you can remove nails that have small heads. (See Figure 1-7 if you're wondering what this tool looks like.)

✔ **Blue painter's tape:** This tape, available in an assortment of widths, protects edges from unwanted spatters and splotches. The tape has a waxy coating that doesn't allow paint to penetrate, and paint can't seep under tape pressed firmly in place. Best of all, if you remove it at the right time, this tape won't damage freshly painted walls. Taping edges takes time, but the reward is taking the tape off and seeing that you have crisp lines where ceilings meet walls and between walls and trim. (Check out this item in Figure 1-8.)

✔ **Clean, dry rags:** Keep these on hand for cleanup and to spot-clean drips of paint.

✔ **Disposable liners:** Use these liners in your paint tray to reduce cleanup time. (Figure 1-10 shows you the liners and the paint tray.)

Figure 1-7: Wooden stir stick, a 5-in-1 tool, and a paint can opener.

Figure 1-8: Blue painter's tape and a dropcloth keep your workspace tidy.

Figure 1-9: Roller cages, extension handles, paint trays, and liners come in handy.

✔ **Dropcloths:** Use these plastic sheets to protect floors and furnishing. (This item is shown in Figure 1-8.) Newspapers work in a pinch.

✔ **Extension handle:** These extensions screw into the handle of roller cages and come in 4- and 8-foot lengths. They let you get into hard-to-reach places and speed up painting flat surfaces, such as walls, ceilings, and floors. You get more control with the shorter length, but you'll have to use a ladder to reach the ceiling or top of walls. (Figure 1-9 shows you this tool.)

✔ **Paint can opener:** You want to use a paint can opener because it won't dent the paint can and the lid — a screwdriver or another makeshift opener might. If the can or lid is damaged, the can won't seal properly and the product can dry out or form a surface skin. (Figure 1-7 shows this tool.)

✔ **Paint tray:** Use a paint tray to load paint onto a roller. Paint trays have wells for holding paint and ribs for distributing and removing excess paint from the roller. Durable metal trays will last for years if you clean them thoroughly. Alternately, you can use inexpensive, disposable plastic liners inside your tray to lengthen its life and for quick cleanup. (See Figure 1-9.)

✔ **Permanent black marker:** Keep one handy to write on the lids of the containers you use for storing paint. Write the date, the name of the paint, where it was used, and the mixing formula.

Selecting a quality brush

If you've ever painted anything with a cheap brush, you know that the bristles come off. You find them floating in the paint and stuck on the walls. The bristles on a cheap brush are stiff and very likely to leave bristle marks on wet surfaces. A quality brush has flexible bristles that don't fall out. It costs much more than a cheap brush, but it's worth every penny because you don't get frustrated by debris left on the wet paint and you don't have to waste time picking it out. And the flexible bristles allow you to use the brush at any angle. A quality brush is easier to clean and can be used repeatedly if you clean it thoroughly and hang it up while the bristles dry.

You can choose from natural and synthetic bristles. Synthetics — such as nylon or a nylon/polyester blend — can be used with latex, oil-based, or alkyd paints, and all types of varnishes. They're easy to clean; the bristles don't get soft or misshapen while you're working. Never use a natural bristle brush with latex paint; natural fibers soak up water, and latex has a water-based formula. Natural bristle brushes, usually hog bristles or ox hair, are soft and spread oil-based paint smoothly and evenly.

✔ **Plastic spray bottle and water:** Use this combo to clean up latex paint splotches.

✔ **Roller cage:** You need this tool to support the roller cover. (See Figure 1-9 for an example.)

✔ **Supply of old newspapers:** This supply comes in handy as dropcloths or additional protection on furnishings and floors, but note that they don't protect as well as plastic dropcloths. You can also "paint" them to get excess paint off brushes and rollers when you're cleaning them.

✔ **Wood stir sticks:** You need them for mixing paint. Paint stores routinely hand out stir sticks when you buy paint. Even though the paint is well shaken at the store, stir the paint again each time you open the can. (Check out Figure 1-7 to see stir sticks.)

Tools for decorative painting

Faux finishes and other decorative paint applications use special tools and glazes as well as the more common tools mentioned earlier in this chapter. Often, specialized tools aren't used for other faux finishes. Paint stores and home improvement centers carry most of the specialized tools. For some finishes, you need only tools you already have — pencils, rulers, yardsticks, and so on. A word of advice: Hang onto those old plastic and paper grocery bags. You can use them to create some finishes. Also keep a good supply of torn or stained t-shirts and cut them up for rags to use while you're painting or cleaning up.

A lot of the projects in this book ask you to apply paint or glaze with these fairly traditional brushes, rollers, and other applicators:

- **2-inch angled sash brush:** Use this brush for leather, stripes, and clouds.

- **2-inch flat sash brush:** This is the brush you want for glazed finishes.

- **3-inch flat sash brush (or colorwashing brush):** Use this brush for color-washing and stippling finishes.

- **3-inch paintbrush:** Use this versatile brush for suede finishes.

- **3-inch wallpaper brush:** Use it to drag glaze off your base coat. You can substitute a dragging brush or wood graining comb if your project has a dragged finish. (See Figure 1-10 to look at this brush.)

- **4-inch flat sash brush:** Use this brush for a gradient finish.

- **12-inch wallpaper brush:** This brush creates chambray, dragging, and metallic finishes. (Figure 1-10 shows this brush as well as a smaller version.)

Figure 1-10: Two wallpaper brushes, a colorwashing brush, and a stippling brush.

- **Artist's brushes:** These brushes come in small, medium, and large sizes. You can choose narrow and round bristled brushes. Select one of these brushes for faux finishes such as stenciling.

- **Mini-roller:** Use the 4- or 6-inch size for dragging, stripes, bagging, checkerboard, and harlequin finishes. If a finish calls for one of these mini-rollers, you need the roller cage and a cover. Don't try to make do with a 9-inch roller because it can't reach into small, tight areas. ***Bonus:*** After you use this roller for a specialty project, you have just the right tool for getting into corners on routine paint projects. (Figure 1-11 shows a mini-roller on a cage.)

- **Sea sponges:** Use these sponges for the sponging off and sponging on projects. Sponging with a sea sponge creates a much more realistic look than any synthetic sponge can provide. (See Figure 1-12 for a glimpse of a sea sponge.)

Selecting a quality roller cover

Along with selecting the right depth of the nap for the project, choose a quality roller cover to get a satisfying finish. A lambskin cover works best if the surface is smooth and when you're using an alkyd or oil-based paint. If you're applying primer, glossy paint, or enamel, look for a mohair cover. For gloss and semi-gloss paint and clear finish coats, a foam rubber cover also does a good job. Foam rollers are easy to use and clean, but if you load too much paint on one, it drips. A roller's ability to hold paint and apply it evenly depends on the density of the nap. Because inexpensive rollers tend to get matted, paint will look uneven or patchy if the roller sheds lint that sticks to the paint, even if you're using quality paint.

Figure 1-11: A mini-roller and a larger suede roller.

✔ **Sheepskin pad:** This tool is your best bet for creating a cloud finish. Don't improvise — you can't create the same look with other tools. (Figure 1-12 shows this natural tool.)

✔ **Shower squeegee:** Notch the squeegee and use it as a guideline in marking the wall for a wavy stripe finish. (Check out Figure 1-12 for details.)

✔ **Small artist's liner brush:** Use this brush for fine detailing in stencil finishes. (See Figure 1-13 for one of these brushes.)

Figure 1-12: A sheepskin pad, a sea sponge, a shower squeegee, and a large steel trowel.

Figure 1-13: Use a small artist's brush or a stencil brush for detail work.

- **Small chip brush:** Use this brush for stippling, bagging, and colorwashing finishes. You should also try this brush when you need to get paint into tight areas or fill voids in the colorwashing and stippling finishes.

- **Small wiz roller:** This roller is best for ragging. It has numerous tiny pieces of cloth that flap onto the surface you're finishing. It's a lot like a mini version of what you see in a car wash.

- **Steel trowel:** Use this tool to apply Venetian plaster to your walls. (Figure 1-12 shows you an example of this tool.)

- **Stencil brush:** Naturally, you want to use one of these when you're stenciling. This brush helps you pounce the stencil pattern onto your wall. (Figure 1-13 shows this brush.)

- **Stippling brush:** Use this brush dry on your finish coat to create a multitude of tiny points of base color. It's also your best bet for stippling and colorwashing finishes. You can use a dry 3-inch flat sash brush as a substitute. (Flip back to Figure 1-10 for a look at this brush.)

- **Suede roller:** Use this specialized roller only with suede paint to create a suede finish. (See Figure 1-11.)

Some of the tools you need for decorative painting are everyday items that you wouldn't necessarily associate with painting. You probably have lots of the items in this list already, and the ones you don't have are easily obtainable:

- **Blank newsprint:** You can pick up this material at an office supply store; it's used in flip charts. Use it when you're doing a frottage finish.

- **Brown paper bags or heavy-weight brown mailing paper:** Use either of these for the frottage technique.

- **Clean rags and terry cloth towels:** You use these for almost all paint finishes. Recycle old t-shirts by turning them into clean rags and keep a good supply on hand. (They make great dust cloths, too, if you dampen them slightly with water.) The terry cloth towels are used for colorwashing, ragging off, and glazing techniques.

- **Disposable plastic plates:** These everyday items are perfect disposable paint palettes.

✔ **Heavy-weight plastic bag:** This is another tool you can use for the frottage finish.

✔ **Heavy-weight sheet of solid plastic:** Use this tool to encourage your inner artist and create your own stencil design.

✔ **Hobby knife:** Use this knife to cut out stencils. A utility knife works well too.

✔ **Level:** Use a level when you're creating pattern finishes, such as stripes, stencils, color blocks, checkerboard, harlequin, and for dragging (including grasscloth, denim, and linen) finishes.

✔ **Pencils:** Make sure you have both plain and colored pencils for marking patterns and lines before you start painting.

✔ **Plain white tissue paper:** This is a key tool if you want a crumpled tissue paper finish on your walls.

✔ **Plastic grocery bags:** This tool gives the bagging technique its name.

✔ **Plastic wrap:** Use this as an alternate for grocery bags in the bagging technique.

✔ **Scissors:** For cutting sponges and paper patterns for stencils.

✔ **White poster board:** Use this for trying out paint and glaze combinations and practicing finishing techniques before you start any of the projects.

✔ **Yardstick, tape measure, and ruler:** For measuring patterns and marking walls so that you know where to apply certain finishes and colors.

If you're interested in a faux finish or other decorative techniques, you may need some of the following glazes, varnishes, and adhesives. Water-based latex glazes can be used only on top of latex paint. However, oil-based glazes can be used on both latex and alkyd paint. Because oil-based glazes dry slower than latex glazes, you have more time to work on complex finish designs. Oil-based glazes generally have a rich, warm hue and therefore aren't well suited to finish white or pastel colors.

✔ **Acrylic glaze:** Provides a transparent, slightly tinted finish pattern over latex base paint. This glaze, like the latex paint, is water-based.

✔ **Acrylic gloss varnish:** Water-based varnish provides a hard, non-yellowing, glossy seal coat on latex glazes. Use it to keep finishes from being chipped or scratched.

✔ **Acrylic spray varnish:** Spray this water-based sealer on porous or large surfaces, such as the top of a table or chest of drawers, to give them a durable finish. Use with latex glazes to prevent water marks, chips, and scratches.

✔ **Crackle glaze:** Using a glaze that's one shade off the base color gives the finished surface a subtle crackled effect.

✔ **Matte acrylic varnish:** When you don't want a shiny surface that reflects light, using this product gives you a subtle, yet hard, protective coat. It intensifies dull colors and isn't removable.

✔ **Metallic glaze:** Metallic finishes give base coats a soft, radiant glow. You can get an elegant patina, a brushed metal finish, or a naturally weathered look that you'd find on cast iron furnishings and accessories.

✔ **Ready-to-use wallpaper adhesive:** Use this roll-on adhesive to seal tissue paper finishes to the wall.

✔ **Spray adhesive:** This adhesive holds the stencil pattern in place while you paint the designs on the wall, and then releases the pattern easily. You may see it labeled as stencil spray adhesive.

Tools for cleanup

No one enjoys cleaning up after a paint project, but manufacturers have designed products to take some of the burden off cleaning up brushes, rollers, and paint trays. Supplies that will help you with the cleanup chore include

✔ **Krud Kutter:** This product is a cleanser that works well on latex glaze cleanup.

✔ **Mild liquid soap:** Use the same stuff you use in the kitchen to clean up latex paint.

✔ **Mineral spirits or paint thinner:** When you're ready to clean up alkyd or oil-based paint and varnish finishes, use mineral spirits or paint thinner. You can also prep your roller cover with thinner when you're using oil-based paints. Both mineral spirits and paint thinner do the job well, but a container of mineral spirits is kinder to your wallet.

✔ **Paint strainer or cheesecloth:** Either of these tools helps you strain debris out of leftover paint. You'll want to do that before you reuse the paint for touch ups or other projects.

✔ **Rubber mallet:** Use this tool to close paint can lids. A regular hammer will do if you tap gently.

✔ **Small empty paint cans:** Recycle your empty paint cans by using them to store excess paint in an airtight container. Dab a dot of paint on the lid, and write the color and mixing code on the lid with permanent marker. Then you know what's in the paint can without opening it and exposing the paint to air. A small lidded plastic bucket works as well.

✔ **Wire brush or comb:** These items remove excess paint from a paintbrush before you clean it.

Extras worth considering

Some other tools aren't required but can make paint projects much simpler. Consider the following tools before you start your next paint job:

✔ **Brush and roller spinner:** These tools are great for cleaning up latex paint and then for removing excess water from your brushes and rollers after you clean them. (See Figure 1-14.) Spin brushes and rollers into a large cardboard box or bucket to contain any spatter.

Figure 1-14: A pour spout, squirrel attachment, brush and roller spinner, pad painter, and paint guard.

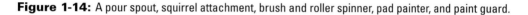

- ✔ **Electric finishing sander:** Use this tool to smooth surfaces quicker than you can with elbow grease.

- ✔ **Foam pad painters in various shapes and sizes:** Whether washable or disposable, these foam pad painters come in handy when you need to paint into tight corners. The smaller pad is best for those corners, while a larger pad is great for painting paneled doors. Whatever size you choose, the pad painter looks like a paintbrush whose bristles have been replaced by a foam sponge.

- ✔ **Liquid chemical deglosser:** This product dulls the surface of glossy paint; use it before applying latex paint over a glossy paint.

- ✔ **Metal paint guard:** This tool guarantees that when you're painting edges on the wall, the brush won't smear paint on the ceiling, floor, or trim by accident. (Check out Figure 1-14.)

- ✔ **Pour spout for paint can:** A pour spout makes pouring paint into a roller tray or bucket less messy and can prevent unwanted spills. (Figure 1-14 shows this handy tool.)

- ✔ **Squirrel paint mixer electric drill attachment:** If you have a drill, this attachment helps mix paint to avoid settlement. If you don't have one, use a stir stick. (See Figure 1-14 for a look at this attachment.)

Narrowing Down Your Paint Options

All paint products have one of two common bases — water or oil. The base gives paint particular characteristics that come into play when you're selecting a finish, getting the right brushes and rollers, and cleaning up afterward. The following sections give you the pros and cons of latex and alkyd paint, and tell you about all the various sheens you can choose from when you're selecting the best paint for your project.

Deciding on latex or alkyd

Latex paints are now formulated to dry within as little as an hour, which homeowners like because they can put the room back together much more quickly. But when you're painting, you have a smaller window for taking breaks because of the quick drying time. And washing latex may cause the finish to look streaky or uneven when it's dry. Water-based latex paint is also popular with do-it-yourselfers because you can clean brushes, rollers, and paint trays quickly with common household products; all you need is a mild dishwashing detergent and water. You can remove unintended splotches of paint as you work by wiping them off with a damp cloth. Latex provides a flat, dull surface that can look sophisticated and elegant, unlike the shine of glossy oil-based paint. But dry latex finishes aren't as easily cleaned or scrubbed as oil-based paint.

Oil-based and alkyd paints dry slowly — in 12 or more hours — and have much more sheen or gloss than water-based paint gives you. They're durable, sanitary, and have a hard finish that can be scrubbed and cleaned without worrying about leaving streaks. You need paint thinner or mineral spirits to clean up mistakes, and to clean up the brushes and rollers you use to apply alkyd or oil-based paint. That's not so bad when you're dipping a paintbrush into a can filled with paint thinner, but removing paint from a roller and cover is messy.

Most homeowners, therefore, prefer latex paint for most projects. They can use one of the finishes that has enough sheen to be cleanable. (See the next section for a discussion on sheen.)

Selecting a paint sheen

The sheen — how bright or shiny the paint looks when it dries — varies according to different paint products. Latex paint looks dull in comparison to shinier oil-based paints because latex paint tends to absorb light while glossy paint reflects it. Along with the way the finished project looks, sheen determines how well the finish holds up to finger marks and crayon, and how easily it shows imperfections. It determines the ambiance of a room, whether it's sophisticated and elegant or utilitarian in appearance. The look, durability, and ambiance you want generally determine which particular paint is best for you.

Just because oil paints are naturally shinier than latex paints, however, doesn't mean that you can't get a nice sheen with the more user-friendly latex paint. Manufacturers give latex paint varying grades or levels of sheen — those levels also determine how cleanable the paint is. The following list tells you more about some of the sheens, and Figure 1-15 shows you some of the different sheens side by side. *Note:* Names and choices may vary, depending on the manufacturer.

   ✔ **Flat latex paint** has an opaque finish that looks elegant on interior walls and ceilings. It's also the most dense, or most light absorbing, of all the paint choices. It doesn't clean well and isn't suited for kitchens, baths, or children's bedrooms. If you have children in the house, just know that the only way to get rid of finger marks and scribbles on this finish is to paint over them.

✔ **An eggshell finish** provides a low luster on interior walls and is used for many decorative finishes. It cleans up better than matte and flat paint, but we recommend more sheen in the paint you use in kitchens and bathrooms.

✔ **Satin finish,** which has more sheen than an eggshell finish, cleans even better than the finishes that make up the beginning of this list. It's a good choice for woodwork, walls, doors, and hallways. You can use it in a bathroom or kitchen if you prefer not to use a glossy paint — but satin isn't as scrubbable as the glossy paints.

✔ **Semi-gloss paint** gives a shiny look to a room, but it's not as shiny as a high-gloss paint. It's scrubbable and good for moldings, doors, windows, kitchens, and baths.

✔ **A high-gloss finish** reflects the most light and definitely shines. But it's also stain resistant and scrubbable, which makes it a good choice for kitchens and baths — the areas of a home that get the most wear and tear. When you use this finish, you don't have to worry about a tomato (whole or in ketchup form) crashing to the floor and spraying up on the wall, and even a cola or wine stain will clean up easily.

One caveat: When you're deciding on which sheen you want to use, remember the higher the sheen, the darker and more intense the color will be.

| Flat | Eggshell | Satin | Semi-gloss | High-gloss |

Figure 1-15: Compare the various sheens and decide which works best for you.

Determining How Much Paint You Need

Whether you paint an entire room, a single wall, or a section (or all) of your floor, you want to make sure that you have enough paint to finish the project you start. Figure out how much paint you need by using the formulas in this section. Determining the amount of paint you need before you start is especially important for larger rooms. You want each gallon you purchase to be consistent in color; this consistency is easier to achieve if you purchase all your paint at the same time. Use the handy table on the Cheat Sheet in the front of this book to keep track of how much paint you need.

You get what you pay for. If you want to cover your walls with just one coat, purchase quality paint even though it costs more than some brands on the market. If you choose a cheaper option, you may find that, ultimately, you have to purchase several gallons of paint and go over the walls several times to get good coverage.

For walls

You usually can't return unused cans of custom mixed paint, so if you buy too many, you have to store the excess, paint another room the same color, give away what you don't use, or hope your local store will let you exchange the unopened paint cans for another color. At the same time, having a partial gallon sitting around is nice — you can later use the paint to touch up marred walls. Just make sure you accurately estimate how much you need so you aren't surprised when you have too much, or too little, paint.

To determine what it will take to coat the walls once, use the following formula:

1. **Add together the length of each wall.**

   For example, 16 + 16 + 20 + 20 = 72 feet

2. **Multiply the total length of walls by the total height.**

   72 feet × 9 feet = 648 square feet

3. **Subtract 20 square feet per door and 15 square feet per window.**

   648 − 20 − 20 − 20 − 15 − 15 − 15 − 15 = 528 square feet

4. **Divide the answer by 350 (the estimated coverage/gallon) for smooth walls; divide by 300 for rough or textured walls, which soak up more paint.**

   528 ÷ 350 = 1.5 gallons for smooth walls

   528 ÷ 300 = 1.76 gallons for rough/textured walls

For floors and ceilings

If you're painting a smooth ceiling or floor, all you have to do is calculate the square footage of the surface. Note that rough surfaces, however, reduce the square footage covered by a gallon of paint. Read the information provided by the manufacturer to determine how much paint you'll need for a rough surface. Just follow these steps to determine how much paint you need for smooth floors and ceilings:

1. **Multiply the length of the floor or ceiling by the width of the floor or ceiling.**

   For example, 16 × 20 = 320 square feet

2. **Divide your answer by 350 (estimated coverage per gallon).**

   320 ÷ 350 = 0.914 gallons

Chapter 2

Readying Your Room and Surface

Preparing a room or surface for painting isn't brain surgery — it's just good common sense. Preparation can involve a number of tasks from patching peeling paint to sealing and priming the surface. Approaching these tasks fully prepared to do them well ensures that the painting job will go smoothly and that the results will be rewarding.

Other than the essential tools (which we list for you in a quick and easy checklist at the start of each project), the only key component you need is patience. Even though you may be chomping at the bit to pull out your paintbrushes, remember: Failing to properly prepare is not a shortcut, but an invitation to disaster.

Painting over wallpaper

Sometimes painting over a wallcovering is the right — and only — thing to do, and you've probably seen plenty of decorating shows on television do it. So when is it okay to paint over wallpaper? In these circumstances:

✔ When the paper was hung ages ago

✔ When the paper was installed over unprimed drywall

✔ When the paper hides holes

✔ When you don't have the time or energy needed to do the massive fixes

If you decide to paint over paper, you need to prepare before you roll on your finish coat. Follow these steps:

1. **Make sure seams are snug.**

2. **Smooth out the surface and give it some tooth by sanding it with 150-grit sandpaper.**

3. **Dust (or vacuum) the surface.**

4. **Brush on two thin coats of oil-based sealer.**

After you follow these steps, you're ready to roll on your finish coat.

Safeguarding the Area

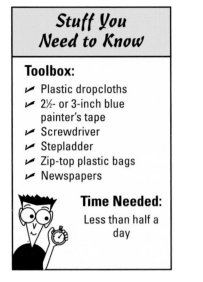

Stuff You Need to Know

Toolbox:

- Plastic dropcloths
- 2½- or 3-inch blue painter's tape
- Screwdriver
- Stepladder
- Zip-top plastic bags
- Newspapers

Time Needed:
Less than half a day

An ounce of prevention truly is worth a pound of cure! For example, it's far easier to throw a protective dropcloth over a velvet sofa and floors than to try to remove a paint spatter from the upholstery and carpet. Similarly, taping is the easy way to mask off any surface that needs to be protected from paint from a wayward brush or roller or spillover of a cleaning liquid. Areas generally taped off are baseboards, ceiling moldings, window and door frames, and electrical switches and outlets. If you're painting trim, tape off edges of surrounding walls to avoid having to touch up the wall or repaint the entire room.

Here's a cool tip: Mover's coasters are handy tools; place them under the feet of a piece of furniture in order to make it slide easily.

1. Remove furniture from the room. If you can't remove some heavy or bulky pieces, cluster them in the center of the room, leaving space to walk around (and through the furniture cluster if you plan to paint the ceiling).

2. Cover the furniture with one or more plastic dropcloths (plastic because it's paint-resistant). Using painter's tape, tape the dropcloths in place, either to the back of furniture or to the floor.

3. Cover the floor with one or more plastic dropcloths. Tape it down with blue painter's tape to avoid slippage.

4. Use a screwdriver to remove all window treatments, including draperies, rods, shutters, blinds, shades, and all hardware. Place the hardware in a zip-top bag for safekeeping.

5. Starting at one corner of the top of a window or door frame, align a piece of blue painter's tape with the edge or strip of the molding that meets the wall.

6. Bring the tape across the window or door frame, pressing it into place as you go. Tape all around the frame.

7. Repeat Steps 5 and 6 around all window and door frames in the room as well as along any trim and baseboards.

8. Switch off lights in the room and then unscrew and remove all electrical faceplates — switches and outlets. Place the screws and coordinating faceplates in a zip-top bag.

9. Cover exposed outlets and switches with blue painter's tape. Tape wall switches in a closed position so that no one inadvertently turns on the overhead fan or light.

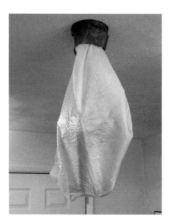

10. If you're painting a ceiling, make sure ceiling-hung light fixtures and overhead fan switches are in a closed position, and then cover the fixture with a piece of plastic dropcloth that you've cut to fit and taped in place.

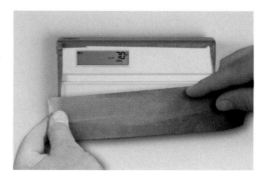

11. Depending on the time of year, turn down the thermostat for heat or raise the setting for air conditioning to kick on in order to reduce the amount of air and dust circulating through ducts. The dust can cling to wet paint.

12. Cover the thermostat with blue painter's tape to keep it paint-free.

If it's necessary to protect the face (front) of a window frame (or perhaps a mirror in a bathroom), tape newspapers or a sheet of plastic over it.

Don't be tempted to use masking tape instead of blue painter's tape. Paint can bleed under masking tape because it doesn't stick to the taped surface as well as painter's tape. And you may not realize it until after you pull the masking tape off.

Removing Scrubbable Wallpaper

Stuff You Need to Know

Toolbox:

- ✔ Bucket or large spray bottle
- ✔ Scoring or perforating tool for scrubbable wallpaper
- ✔ Plastic dropcloths
- ✔ Screwdriver
- ✔ Wallpaper remover solution
- ✔ Sponge
- ✔ Wallboard knife
- ✔ TSP or TSP-PF

Time Needed:
About a weekend

Wallpaper that's hung well is hung to stay, or so it seems when you try to take it down! Ease of removal depends on the type of wallpaper you're dealing with. For example, some types of wallpaper, such as vinyl, are easy to pull off walls but that's only the top layer. They leave behind a paper lining and glue residue that you have to spend some time scrubbing off. Scrubbable wallpaper, which is covered in this project, is a common wallcovering with a coating that requires the additional step of scoring for removal.

If you have vinyl wallpaper, skip Steps 3 through 7. Instead, look for a loose corner seam or gently insert the edge of a putty knife under a lower corner at the seam to lift the edge of the vinyl paper. Be careful that you grab the finish layer, leaving the paper backing on the wall. Gently lift the wallpaper strip up and out. Don't yank the paper off; if you do, you may tear off the paper backing and parts of the wall. Use the putty knife, if needed, to separate the finish layer from the backing. Continue these steps until you remove all the strips, and then head to Step 8.

The time needed to complete this project depends on several factors, including the size of the room, the number of wallpaper strips you need to remove, and the stubbornness of the wallpaper glue. Remove the first strip of wallpaper and then estimate the total time needed for the rest of the project.

1. Test whether the wallpaper is scrubbable by spraying an area with water. If the water beads up and runs down the wall, your paper is scrubbable and you need to use the scoring or perforating tool.

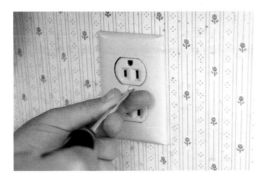

2. Cover the floor with plastic dropcloths, and use a screwdriver to remove faceplates and outlet covers (turn the power off first to be safe).

If the faceplates are covered with wallpaper, drop them into a bucket of water to soak while you remove paper from the wall.

3. Score the wallpaper with the scoring or perforating tool, using a circular or twisting motion of your hand so that the cutting edge penetrates the paper. Take care not to press down too hard, especially if the scoring tool has spikes; you may puncture the wall and have to repair it. Work up and down or across the paper, getting in close at corners.

4. Prepare the wallpaper remover solution according to the manufacturer's instructions, and then spray on the remover solution or use a sponge and bucket to wet the surface of the wallpaper. The scoring from Step 3 allows the solution to penetrate the paper and soften the glue.

5. When the adhesive has softened, which should take 15 to 30 minutes, start at a seam, with a wallboard knife in one hand, and pry the paper loose from the wall. Pull the paper up gently with the other hand as you go. You may have to work the knife under the edges to loosen them.

6. Repeat Steps 4 and 5 until you remove all strips of wallpaper.

7. When all the strips are down, go over the wall again with the wallboard knife to remove any torn fragments of paper.

8. Remove all traces of paste using a damp sponge and either a TSP or TSP-PF solution or wallpaper removal product (most types dissolve the paste, but you should check the manufacturer's instructions to be sure).

Some wallpaper glue can be especially stubborn. If you can't dissolve yours, sand the walls with 220-grit sandpaper to remove the glue, and then wash the walls down with a TSP solution (see Chapter 1).

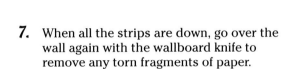

If the manufacturer's instructions on the wallpaper removal solution say to wipe off the product and paste with a damp sponge, be careful not to get the wall too wet. The wall must be completely dry before you paint it.

Repairing Peeling Paint on Woodwork and Trim

Stuff You Need to Know

Toolbox:
- ✔ 2-inch blue painter's tape and dropcloth (optional)
- ✔ 5-in-1 tool
- ✔ 180-grit sandpaper
- ✔ Tack cloth
- ✔ Clean rags
- ✔ Premixed, tinted wood filler (if needed)

Time Needed:

About a weekend, depending on how much woodwork needs to be repaired

You can find peeling paint on woodwork throughout the house, and baseboards are no exception. Children and pets can damage the paint on your baseboards without much effort; they don't mean any harm, but you're left with flaking paint that needs to be fixed.

Another common cause of peeling paint on your woodwork — particularly windowsills — is moisture. If your woodwork has water damage, make sure you find the source of the problem first. Tackle that problem, and then sand or strip the trim down to the bare wood. Prime and paint the wood following the directions in the projects on priming and painting baseboards, molding, and trim (see Chapter 9).

1. To avoid getting paint chips and dust on your floor, tape a dropcloth below the baseboard. Or you can vacuum up any debris after Step 5 and Step 8.

2. Use a hook-type paint scraper or 5-in-1 tool to gently scrape away loose, chipping paint. Use very light pressure, taking care not to gouge the wood surface, and scrape down to the bare wood if necessary.

3. If water has raised the grain of the wood underneath (you can tell because the wood will be bumpy), take off enough paint to expose adjacent undamaged wood. Use 180-grit sandpaper to sand the damaged spot until the wood itself is smooth.

4. Feather the edges of adjoining paint with sandpaper so that the painted and unpainted areas feel even and smooth.

5. Wipe off dust with a tack cloth or damp rag, and vacuum any paint chips that are on the floor.

6. If the wood has any gouges or dented areas, fill them with wood filler and let it dry.

7. Sand dry wood filler with sandpaper until the surface is smooth.

8. Wipe off dust with a tack cloth or damp rag.

9. Seal, prime, and paint the wood, following the directions in the projects on priming and painting baseboards, molding, and trim in Chapter 9.

Stripping Paint from Wood Trim

Stuff You Need to Know

Toolbox:

- Chemical stripper
- 2-inch blue painter's tape (or wider tape)
- Newspaper (optional)
- Goggles
- Breathing mask
- Latex gloves
- Old 2-inch paintbrush
- Putty knife (or plastic scraper)
- Steel wool pads
- Old toothbrush or any other small, stiff-bristled brush for grooves and corners
- Denatured alcohol
- Sponge

Time Needed:
About a weekend

Stripping paint can be a very satisfying project because you see almost instantaneous results. But it's important to take precautions when working with strong chemicals such as strippers. Always work in a well-ventilated room, keep doors open, and even on a cold day, crack open a nearby window for a source of fresh air. A breathing mask cuts down on the fumes you're exposed to, but you should also ventilate the space.

Before you begin, open the windows and doors of the room you're working in. Don goggles, a breathing mask, and protective gloves so that you can safely handle chemicals.

1. Tape the walls above and around the trim. You may also want to protect your floor with a thick layer of newspapers.

2. Read the directions on the container of chemical stripper that you've selected to use. Following the product directions, use an old paintbrush to apply the stripper to the surface of painted trim. Work in a small section of trim to get a feel for the amount of time it takes for the paint to lift and peel off easily; you can increase the size of the section as you proceed around the room.

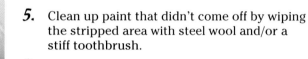

3. Let the stripper set according to the package instructions or until you see the paint beginning to bubble up. (If you let the stripper set too long, it will dry on the trim and be unworkable.) After the paint has bubbled up and while the stripper is still wet, use a putty knife or a plastic scraper to scrape the paint off the surface. Take care not to gouge the scraper into the softened wood.

4. If the trim has layers of paint on it, repeat Steps 2 and 3 as many times as necessary in order to get down to the wood.

5. Clean up paint that didn't come off by wiping the stripped area with steel wool and/or a stiff toothbrush.

6. Dip a fresh, paint-free piece of steel wool into denatured alcohol and rub the area again to remove all traces of paint.

7. Wipe down the paint-free wood trim with a damp sponge.

8. Repeat Steps 2 through 7 on all trim in the room.

Make sure that the trim is completely dry before painting or staining it.

Repairing Woodwork and Trim

Regardless of whether your ultimate goal is to paint it, stain it, or leave it au naturel, old, scarred wood shouldn't pose a problem. Cleaning and repairing dinged or otherwise damaged woodwork — whether it's stained or painted — is an easy project for which you need only some basic skill, tools, and materials. This project focuses on eliminating scratches and dings.

1. Rub steel wool gently over superficial scratches, following the grain of the wood as shown here. For deeper scratches and dings, sand the area with 220-grit sandpaper, following the grain of the wood.

2. Use a rag to rub the area with mineral spirits.

3. Use your fingertip to fill a scratch or ding with premixed wood filler that matches the stain on the rest of the wood.

4. Allow the filler to dry, and then use 220-grit sandpaper to sand the filled area.

5. Wipe down the area with a damp rag or tack cloth to remove dust.

6. Refinish the wood as described in the projects on priming and painting baseboards, molding, and trim.

When it dries, wood putty doesn't absorb stain evenly, which means that tinted, premixed wood filler is the best choice for spot repairs on woodwork.

Filling Nail Holes in the Wall

Stuff You Need to Know

Toolbox:
- ✔ Patching compound
- ✔ Putty knife
- ✔ 120- or 180-grit sandpaper
- ✔ Vacuum cleaner with brush attachment
- ✔ Sponge

Time Needed:
Less than an hour (for one hole)

It always seems as if the smallest nails leave big holes in drywall. The good news is that getting rid of them is simple. Follow these easy steps and you'll be ready to paint the room and rehang the pictures for a completely fresh look in your home.

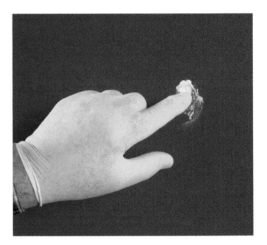

1. Use your fingertip to dab a bit of patching compound into the nail hole.

2. Use a putty knife to scrape the patching compound smooth and flat with the surrounding wall. Let it dry.

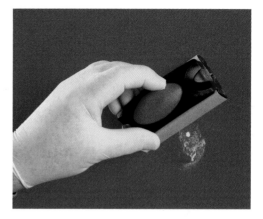

3. Sand the compound area lightly using fine-grit sandpaper and a circular motion until the patch blends in smoothly with the wall. You can test whether it's smooth and even with your fingers.

4. Vacuum the sanded area to remove dust.

5. Wipe the area lightly with a damp sponge, and let the patch dry completely before brushing on primer.

Removing mildew

Mildew stains are caused by airborne mold spores that flourish wherever there's moisture, darkness, and little air movement. In order to get rid of the stain, you have to kill the spores. You can use any of a number of commercial mildewcides available from home improvement or hardware stores, or you can opt for a common home remedy that involves washing the stain with common household laundry bleach.

If you want to try the home remedy, don your rubber gloves and mix a solution of equal parts water and laundry bleach. Wash the stained area with the solution. Wait 30 minutes, and wash it again. If that doesn't do the trick, try a solution of TSP or TSP-PF. Wear protective clothing and goggles, and read the manufacturer's instructions. Make sure you thoroughly sponge your walls with clean water after using the TSP or TSP-PF. Any residue will prevent paint from bonding to the surface.

Finally, when the area is completely dry and stain-free, apply a sealer or primer that contains mildewcide, and then paint it.

Cleaning Surfaces

The only grease that a surface needs before you paint it is elbow grease! Well-washed walls that are free of grease and grime and smooth as silk are an absolute must for ensuring that your paint project proceeds as it should and you get the results you want and expect. Trisodium phosphate (TSP) — or TSP-PF in communities where phosphates are prohibited — is a favorite chemical for washing walls because it gets the job done without creating suds.

1. While wearing protective clothing, gloves, and goggles, dilute the TSP or TSP-PF in water according to the manufacturer's instructions.

2. Dip a sponge into the bucket of TSP solution, squeeze out excess water, and start washing the walls from the bottom up to avoid streaking.

3. Thoroughly rinse the TSP from the bucket and sponge, and then fill the bucket with clear, warm water.

4. Sponge the walls thoroughly with clear water. You want to remove all traces of TSP because any residue will prevent paint from bonding to the surface.

WARNING!

If you have allergies or are sensitive to strong chemicals, ask your paint dealer to recommend a TSP substitute. TSP contains sodium meta-silicate, which may cause burns or irritation and is harmful if swallowed. It's not recommended for use on glossy paint or enamel, and it can darken oak, mahogany, and other woods. If you decide to use it, follow the manufacturer's directions carefully and keep powder and solution out of reach of children.

Priming Baseboards, Molding, and Trim

Before painting, you need to prime all trim; a coat of regular wood primer helps paint adhere whereas a combination sealer-primer keeps stains from showing through and provides an undercoat for the paint. The priming step is especially necessary for trim that has been stained previously or has problems such as knots or discoloration. For new, unfinished wood, you can prime and paint the trim on sawhorses before installing it.

1. Lightly sand the entire surface using 220-grit sandpaper and long, even strokes. Use smaller pieces of sandpaper to get into more ornate or carved surfaces.

2. Wipe off any residue with a clean, damp rag or tack cloth and follow up with a dry rag. Vacuum any dust or debris.

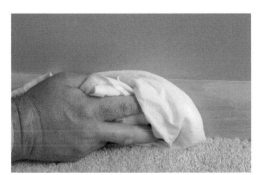

3. In addition to using a paint guard (see Step 5), you can tape the walls adjacent to trim with blue painter's tape (refer to taping instructions earlier in the chapter) to protect them from unintended spatters and brush strokes. If you're painting a baseboard, you can also tape a dropcloth below the board to help keep paint off your floor.

4. Dip one-third of the sash brush's bristles into primer. Tap the brush handle on the side of the can or container to cast off extra primer.

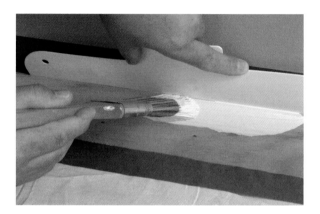

5. Hold a paint guard in one hand, and cover the wall or floor adjacent to the trim you're working on. Brush primer on the woodwork using long strokes.

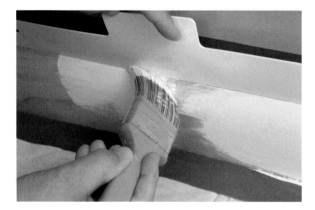

6. Repeat Step 4, and start the next stroke by overlapping the edge of the one you just finished. Blending the edges of wet primer gives you a smoother, more even result.

7. Check periodically for drips. Gently "tap" up any drips by holding the bristle end of a dry brush on the drip, just lightly touching the drip. (The drip will flow — or tap — back into the bottom of the brush.) Don't push the bristles any lower than the surface of the drip.

8. Allow the primer to dry for 24 hours or according to the manufacturer's instructions. Remove any tape from the walls.

Applying Sealer and Primer

To enhance the beauty and durability of freshly painted walls, prep work is necessary. After you clean the walls, as we explain in the "Cleaning Surfaces" project, your next step is to apply a sealer and/or primer. This project tells you how to apply sealer to a water-stained area of a wall or wood trim and how to prime the walls. If you're using a sealer to cover a water stain on a wall or ceiling, make sure that the source of the water (like condensation from an air conditioner, leaking pipe, or hole in the roof) has been repaired and that the stained surface is dry and firm. If you don't need to seal anything, follow Step 1 and then skip to Step 6.

1. Open doors and windows (at least a crack in cold weather) to ventilate the room.

2. Dip a 2½-inch sash brush into the can of sealer, tapping the brush against the can to remove excess sealer.

3. Brush sealer onto the stained area of the wall, and then let it dry completely.

4. Sand sealed surface with 180-grit sandpaper until smooth, feathering out edges. This is especially important with water stains because as water soaks in, it expands drywall, and on wood, moisture leaves a rough surface after drying. You also want the surface smooth before applying finish paint.

5. Use the brush attachment on your vacuum cleaner to vacuum away any dust and residue from the stained area.

6. Start applying primer in a 3 to 4 foot section of the wall by cutting in the corners with a 2½-inch brush.

7. Roll on primer. Start in the corner and roll an "M" (this roller technique is described in Chapter 4).

8. Wipe up any drips as you go along by wicking up excess primer with a clean, dry brush — just lightly touch the end of the brush to the drip. You can also use a clean dry rag to wick it up; just twist a small area of the rag and lightly touch it to the drip.

9. Continue painting around the room, section by section, working primer from dry areas into wet ones.

10. Wait for the primer to dry (it can take any-where from one to several hours; read the manufacturer's instructions), and then sand any imperfections, such as dust or a drip that has dried, off the wall. Sand lightly with 180-grit sandpaper. If you don't remove imperfections before adding the finish paint, they will be visible until you redo the room again.

11. Use the brush attachment on your vacuum cleaner to vacuum the wall to clean up any sanding dust. If you leave dust on the surface, it will show through the finish coat.

TIP

If you want to spot prime a surface, don't create a square or circular patch because it will be noticeable after you paint the wall. Feather out the primer and the paint. Likewise, if you have to prime multiple spots, prime those spots, and then paint the whole wall.

Chapter 3

Making Necessary Wall Repairs

Tasks performed in this chapter

- Repairing cracks in drywall
- Repairing holes in drywall
- Repairing cracks and small holes in plaster
- Repairing popped nails

Your paint job is only as good as your prep work. And when you're painting walls, the most important prep work you can do is to fix the dings, dents, and other flaws that can't be camouflaged with paint; these flaws can include anything from a small nail hole to a fist-sized hole.

Even though fixing these things may actually take more time than painting does, a few hours spent righting the wrongs will pay off in a perfect paint job. Fortunately, you don't have to be a craftsman to tackle minor repairs to either of the two most common wall surfaces:

- **Drywall** (sometimes referred to as Sheetrock): The most common wall type in housing today, drywall consists of gypsum, a chalky rock, sandwiched between paper. Drywall is sturdy when nailed into place, but it's vulnerable to nicks and knocks. Repairing, happily, requires only basic skills.

- **Plaster walls:** Typically found in pre-WWII homes, plaster walls consist of three layers of plaster applied over *lath* (strips of wood). Although repairing major cracks and large holes in plaster walls requires a professional plasterer, patching small cracks and holes calls only for basic skills, the proper materials and tools, and a fair bit of patience.

With a little know-how and easy-to-follow instructions, you can get your walls in prime shape for painting. The projects in this chapter tell you how.

Repairing Cracks in Drywall

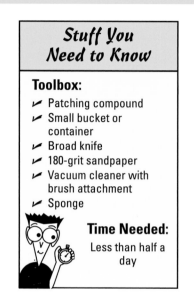
Repairing narrow cracks in drywall requires a thin mix of patching compound (look for one that you mix with water). After the application of just a few thin layers, all you have to do is sand, prime, and paint. Problem solved!

1. Follow the manufacturer's instructions to prepare a thin mix of wall patching compound.

2. Use a broad knife to apply a thin coat of compound (about ¼ inch thick) over the crack.

3. Wipe the broad knife downward over the crack to remove excess compound, and then let the layer dry thoroughly.

4. Repeat Steps 2 and 3 two more times.

5. Use 180-grit sandpaper to sand the patch in a circular motion until the patch feels smooth and level with surrounding walls.

6. Vacuum the sanded patch to remove dust.

7. Wipe the area lightly with damp sponge, and let the patch dry completely before brushing on primer.

Repairing Holes in Drywall

Fixing holes and shallow dents or scratches in drywall with drywall mud creates an even, like-new surface for painting. The tricks are to apply several thin layers of drywall mud into the hole or scratch and to sand them lightly to blend out the edges of the patch and ensure a smooth, even surface. This project addresses both small holes about 1 inch or less in diameter and medium holes about the size of a fist.

Anything larger than a fist-sized hole needs to be patched with a new piece of drywall cut to fit the void. But the job isn't necessarily one that should send you to the phone book to find a handyman or contractor. See *Home Improvement for Dummies* by Gene Hamilton and Katie Hamilton (Wiley) for more info on fixing large holes.

1. Clean out uneven, ragged edges of the hole with a utility knife, and scrape or sand off any pieces of loose drywall or peeled paint.

2. If the hole is deep or goes all the way through the drywall, stuff a piece of fiberglass mesh tape into the hole to provide a base for the drywall mud. Place the mesh over the hole with edges slightly overlapping undamaged drywall.

3. Using a broad knife or your finger (depending on the size of the hole), smooth on about ¼ inch of drywall mud with a downward stroke. Use the broad knife to swipe off any excess mud. (A thin layer of drywall mud dries faster, gives you better control over the repair, and reduces the amount of sanding needed.) Let the patch dry completely.

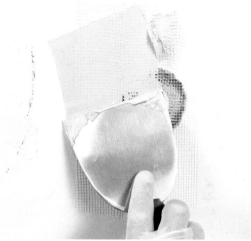

4. Repeat Step 3 two more times or until the patch is level with the wall, taking care to keep each layer thin.

5. Using a 120-grit sanding block, smooth the patch with downward strokes. When the patch is smooth, sand it again using a gentle, circular motion to blend the patch into the rest of the wall.

6. Vacuum the patch to remove dust, and prime the patch before painting.

The process of fixing a dent or nail hole in drywall is essentially the same except that you don't need to use mesh tape because even though it's dented, the drywall backing is still there (and nail holes are usually pretty small).

Repairing Cracks and Small Holes in Plaster

Stuff You Need to Know

Toolbox:

- ✔ Masonry chisel
- ✔ Hammer
- ✔ Screwdriver
- ✔ Bucket
- ✔ Patching compound or patching plaster
- ✔ Electric hand mixer and one beater (or a drill with a mixer attachment)
- ✔ Broad knife
- ✔ 180-grit sandpaper
- ✔ Clean rags

Time Needed:
Less than half a day

Few new homes have plaster walls anymore because installation requires skilled labor and because the settling and drying out that occur as a home ages cause plaster to crack. If you live in an older home that has plaster walls, the good news is that you can easily repair small holes and cracks yourself. The bad news is that you have two choices when it comes to large cracks and holes: Call a specialist to do the difficult repairs, or replace the plaster with drywall.

You can buy plaster patching compound in 3- to 5-pound boxes, which is likely to be enough for your project, but don't worry if you have to buy more than that. The powder will keep for years if it's not exposed to moisture; store it in a tightly covered container or zip-top plastic bag.

1. Use a masonry chisel and hammer to pick at the hole and make it larger. A larger hole takes more patching plaster, which helps it adhere better.

2. Scrape damaged and loose plaster away from the hole with the tip of a screwdriver.

3. In a bucket or small tub, mix powdered plaster patch with water according to the manufacturer's instructions. Use either an electric hand mixer and one beater or a power drill with a mixer attachment, depending on what you have. Don't worry — the plaster patch is water-soluble and washes off easily. *Remember:* When it's exposed to moisture, the patching compound hardens within a couple hours, so mix small quantities several times rather than one big batch.

4. Using a broad knife, fill the crack or hole with the patching compound, and smooth the compound with the flat edge of your knife. (A broad knife works better than a wide-blade putty knife because its sharp edge removes excess plaster and smoothes the patch better.)

5. After the patch is dry, sand it with 180-grit sandpaper, using a circular motion, until it feels smooth and totally flush with the wall.

6. Wipe the patch with a damp rag to remove dust, and let it dry completely before applying primer and paint.

Spot priming and painting works well on ceilings, but not as well on walls because the repaired patches stand out. Plan to repair plaster cracks when you intend to repaint the entire wall.

If you have more than a couple cracks or small holes to repair, mix a small batch of patching compound and repair only two or three of the bad spots. That will give you an idea of how long it takes to do the repair and how long it takes for the compound to harden. And if you find that you work slowly, you won't waste as much compound as you would if you mixed a large batch.

Repairing Popped Nails

Stuff You Need to Know

Toolbox:
- ✔ Electronic stud finder
- ✔ Pencil
- ✔ Screwdriver
- ✔ Drywall screws
- ✔ Hammer
- ✔ Putty knife
- ✔ Patching compound
- ✔ 220-grit sandpaper
- ✔ Vacuum with brush attachment
- ✔ Primer

Time Needed:
Less than half a day

Everyone living with drywall knows about popped nails. Those pesky fasteners make their presence known because the compound covering the nail fails or the head of the nail pokes out above or through the drywall. These faults can occur when a building settles, when nails don't attach to studs, and sometimes just when people walk through a room with bouncy floors. Don't despair if you have popped nails; the repair is fairly simple and makes it easy to give your home a new look without the apparent flaws.

1. Use an electronic stud finder to locate the stud placement around a popped nail. Mark the wall with a pencil when you find a stud. Or you can find the stud by inserting a screw into the wall; if it doesn't hit a stud, move the screw ¼ inch at a time until you do. (Don't worry about multiple holes; you'll patch them later.)

2. Use a screwdriver to fasten drywall screws through the drywall and into the stud slightly above and below the popped nail. Insert the screw far enough that the head is below the wall's surface. Take care not to break through the paper covering the wallboard.

3. Place the pointed tip of a screw on the head of the popped nail and *gently* tap the head of the screw with a hammer. The tapping should dimple the popped nail, sending the head below the surface of the wall. (If you accidentally mar the wall with the hammer, you'll fix it later.)

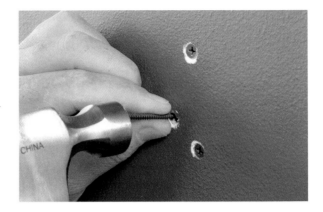

4. Use a putty knife to spread patching compound over the dimpled nails and screws and unwanted screw holes or marred walls, following the manufacturer's instructions. Let the patches dry completely.

5. Repeat Step 4 if needed, and let the patches dry thoroughly.

6. Use 220-grit sandpaper to sand the patches with a circular motion until they feel smooth and level with the wall.

7. Vacuum the patches to remove dust.

8. Apply primer and paint to the patches.

Chapter 4

Brushing Up on Painting Basics

Time-honored, good old-fashioned painting basics still apply today. The choices, quality, and results you can expect from a can of paint have improved tremendously over the years. But prepping the surfaces to be painted hasn't changed. If you want the finished product to look good, the paint still has to be applied to clean, smooth surfaces. So take the time to repaint and wash them well.

"Don't cut corners" is good advice for prepping, but don't mix it up with "cutting *in* corners," the most difficult, frustrating task painters face. In this chapter, you discover ways and products to make these chores easier. The old standards — water and water-based products to clean up latex paint, and paint thinner or mineral spirits to remove alkyd paint — still hold true. But this chapter also has a few new timesaving ideas that reduce your cleanup time.

Lots of people store half-empty paint cans because they know they'll use them for touch ups later. But when they open the can, they see rust on the lid and around the rim. Find out how to eliminate rust and store paint for years — or until you change your color scheme.

In this chapter, you get how-to info for creating flawless finishes, as well as practical techniques for prepping, cleaning, and storing paint.

Prepping Multiple Cans of the Same Color Paint

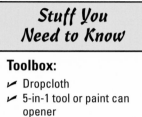

Stuff You Need to Know

Toolbox:

✔ Dropcloth
✔ 5-in-1 tool or paint can opener
✔ Paint (more than one can in the same color)
✔ 5-gallon bucket
✔ Stir sticks designed for 5-gallon buckets

Time Needed:
Less than an hour

You've donned your paint duds, done your prep work — repairing, cleaning, sanding, taping, and draping — and now you're ready to paint. Get your paint project off to a good start by prepping your paint properly.

Paint can vary slightly from can to can, so if you plan to paint a large surface that requires more than one can of paint, ensure color uniformity by *boxing* your paint, the fancy way of saying mixing all the paint together.

1. Cover your work area with a dropcloth, open all your paint cans using a paint can opener or 5-in-1 tool, and then pour the paint into a 5-gallon bucket.

2. Use a large stir stick to stir the paint clockwise for 15 to 30 seconds and then counterclockwise for 15 to 30 seconds. If paint still isn't mixed well enough, stir the paint from front to back for 15 to 30 seconds.

3. To make it more manageable to pour into containers or roller trays, pour the boxed paint from the bucket back into the individual paint cans. Seal all but one can by covering the lids with a rag and tapping around the rim of the lid with a rubber mallet.

4. Pour about 1 inch of paint from the open can into your portable paint container if you're cutting in with a brush or 2 inches of paint in the well of a roller tray if you're ready to roll on paint.

5. Put the lid back on the remaining open can to avoid any accidental spills.

REMEMBER

Paint settles rapidly, so whether you box your paint or not, or whether you just had it stirred at the store, you still need to stir it well before you use it every time.

Making old paint useable again

If your paint has been in storage for a year or more, it may have separated, and lumps may have formed. Even so, you can still save the paint. To do so, you need to remove the lumps and *condition* the paint. Conditioners (sold at paint stores) slow down drying and improve the paint's flow, adhesion, and coverage.

Follow these steps to make your old paint useable again:

1. Skim off any thickened skin on top with an old knife and discard the skin by wrapping it up in newspaper.

2. Stir the paint well or use a paint mixer to break down lumps and mix pigments and other ingredients.

3. Pour paint through a paint strainer or cheesecloth and into a bucket to remove any remaining lumps or debris.

4. Add conditioner to thin the paint and make it spread better and more evenly; conditioner also slows down the quickness with which paint dries. Follow the manufacturer's directions on the conditioner packaging.

5. Stir the paint thoroughly before and while you're using it to keep pigments and other ingredients from separating. If you don't stir, you risk ending up with an uneven appearance on the finish coat.

Voilà! Old paint with new life.

Keeping your can clean

Paint keeps well when it isn't exposed to air. You can keep air exposure to a minimum while you're working. Just pour the approximate amount of paint you need for an hour or so into a smaller container or your roller tray, and put the lid back on the paint can. Some do-it-yourselfers like to get a number of smaller plastic containers; they can be used for mixing paint and as the bucket you dip your brush into.

Air also causes metal paint cans to deteriorate, and that oxidation eventually causes the can to rust. But you can keep the can handy while you're working without buying a gallon's worth of plastic containers. Here are some ways to make paint can prep easier:

✔ **To ease opening:** Use either a 5-in-1 tool or a paint can opener to gently pry up the lid. A paint can opener — a long, narrow stem with a flat, slightly curved edge on one end, and an oval or round head on the other — often is free when you buy paint. Don't use a screwdriver or pointed bottle opener — they could deform the lid, thus making a tight seal

impossible. Keep your paint can closed as much as possible while you're painting. And make sure it's tightly sealed overnight or in storage. These steps will keep paint from drying out, prevent lumps, stop a skin from forming on the surface, and keep air from oxidizing the paint can.

✔ **To make pouring paint easier and cleaner:** Either hammer small holes around the metal rim so that paint drips back into the can, or snap a "duck bill" shaped paint dispenser onto the rim of the can. You can purchase these dispensers wherever you buy paint.

✔ **For convenience and to avoid messes with the lid:** When you first open a paint can, slip the lid into a plastic baggie (medium-sized, zip-closure baggies tend to work best), and put the lid — baggie and all — back onto the paint can until you need to pour more paint. It keeps the paint in the can from drying out and prevents the lid from dripping. When you need to open the can again, just lift the lid by the edge of the plastic baggie.

Cutting In Paint with a Brush

Stuff You Need to Know

Toolbox:

✔ Paint
✔ Small paint container
✔ 2-inch angled sash brush

Time Needed:
Less than half a day

Use brushes to cut in areas that are too tight for rollers (such as at the ceiling line, in corners, and along baseboards and trim) and to apply alkyd paints (brushes tend to leave marks on large surfaces brushed with fast-drying latex paints). See Chapter 1 for a complete discussion of brush types, sizes, and uses.

Prevent trouble before it starts by loading your brush and applying paint the proper way. These simple instructions can help prevent drips and spatter, save your brush for future paint jobs, and produce great-looking results.

1. Pour about 1 inch of paint into your paint container.

2. Hold your brush properly to prevent muscle fatigue in your hand, wrist, and arm. When cutting in, use the pencil grip, which allows for a lot of control. Simply cradle the brush handle between the thumb and index finger of your dominant hand. Rest your index finger on the narrow edge of the brush, and position your thumb on one side and your remaining fingers on the other side of the brush's metal band.

3. Dip your brush bristles straight down into your paint container. The paint should cover only the first third of the bristles. Gently swish and wiggle the brush back and forth in the container to load the brush with paint.

4. Gently tap each side of the brush against the paint container to shake off any excess paint.

5. Make a downward brushstroke on the wall about 2 inches away from the area you want to paint; this placement deposits the excess paint in an open area, making it easier for you to manage, be more precise in the corners, and create a finer line.

6. Turn the brush so that the narrow edge is up, and paint a downward stroke up to 12 inches long in the corner. Applying too much pressure will glop on the paint and make a big drip, so go with a light touch. For long expanses along the ceiling or baseboard, use a horizontal stroke up to 12 inches long.

7. Erase brush marks by turning the brush back so that the wide edge is up, and gently sweeping the brush back over the painted area using light pressure.

8. Repeat Steps 2 through 6, working from dry areas to wet areas and gently overlapping the two sections to avoid marks.

Applying a Base Coat with a Roller

Stuff You Need to Know

Toolbox:

- ✔ Roller cover
- ✔ Roller cage
- ✔ Paint
- ✔ Stir sticks
- ✔ Paint tray and liners
- ✔ Spray bottle filled with water (for latex paint)
- ✔ Paint thinner and tray (for alkyd paint)
- ✔ 5-in-1 tool

Time Needed:

Less than half a day

After you cut in your paint (see the previous project), make fast work of completing your base coat with a roller. Prepping your roller before you douse it in paint ensures even coverage and faster painting — and it saves paint. Properly loading and unloading the roller cuts down on spatter, drips, and spotty coverage. And optimal application techniques, including proper stance, mean fewer touch ups and reduced muscle fatigue.

1. Put your roller cover on the cage. Stir your paint thoroughly with a stir stick, and pour it into the paint tray. You should have only about ½ inch of paint in the well.

2. Dampen the roller cover. For latex (water-based) paint, mist your roller cover with a spray bottle filled with water, or dampen it under a faucet of running water. For alkyd paints, roll the alkyd-appropriate roller cover in a tray of paint thinner. Scrape off excess water or thinner with a 5-in-1 tool.

3. Roll the roller down the slope of the paint tray (called the *rake*) and into the paint well.

4. Evenly distribute the paint on the roller by lifting it up out of well, placing it at the top of the rake, and rolling it downward toward the well but not into it.

5. Repeat Step 4 to evenly load the roller. Take care not to let the roller spin or you'll create spatter. And don't lift the roller out of the tray if any paint is dripping from it.

6. Hold the roller in your dominant hand. If you're using an extension pole, place your dominant hand toward the bottom for control and your nondominant hand at the middle position for leverage and pressure. Stand in front of the wall with your feet shoulder-width apart and your roller directly in front of you for control.

7. Keep the roller cover from flying off the handle by positioning the roller so that the open end points in the direction you're painting. Use a long, slow, upward diagonal stroke to unload the first part of the "M" distribution pattern.

8. In a continuing motion, follow the first upward stroke with a long, slow stroke downward at a diagonal.

9. In a continuing motion, use another long, slow, upward diagonal stroke and another long, slow downward diagonal stroke to finish the "M" pattern.

10. Distribute paint with a series of horizontal strokes starting at the bottom of the "M" and working toward the top.

11. Smooth out the section by rolling vertically downward from top to bottom. At the bottom of each stroke, lift the roller up and return it to the top.

12. Repeat the process of loading the roller and painting, working in sections of three or four roller widths. Move from dry areas to wet ones, overlapping the wet edge each time you start a new section.

TIP

Always use a roller cover with the correct nap length for the job. Luckily, manufacturers put nap length and purpose information right on the package. For example, you usually see ⅜-inch nap roller covers indicated or smooth surfaces and ½-inch nap roller covers for rough surfaces.

Cleaning Water-Based Paint from Brushes

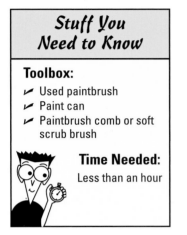
Good brushes can last for years and years. Keep them serviceable by cleaning them properly. Start this task as soon as you're finished with a paintbrush to keep it in the best possible shape.

1. Hold just the paintbrush, and drag it across the top of the paint can, scraping the excess paint back into the can. Reseal the can when you're done.

2. Put the brush under warm running water to rinse out the loose paint. Spread the bristles of the brush to get down into the heel (near the metal band) to clean any paint that may be down there.

3. If any paint remains in or on the brush, use a paintbrush comb or soft scrub brush to remove it. Continue holding the brush under the warm running water while you use this tool.

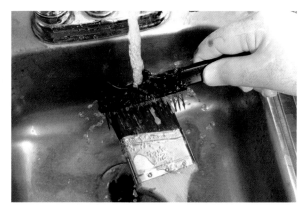

4. Continue to milk the brush from the heel to the end of the bristles. Spread the bristles occasionally until all the paint is gone from the brush and the water coming out of the brush is clear.

5. When the brush is paint-free, take it in one hand and tap the heel of the brush against your other hand repeatedly. This step knocks the water from the brush.

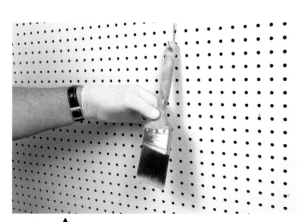

6. Hang the clean, damp paintbrush on a pegboard or place it on a flat surface to dry. When it's dry, place the brush back into its case and store.

TIP

If you've waited several days to clean a brush, try soaking it in warm, soapy water for about 30 minutes before beginning the cleaning process covered in this project. You can also check a paint or home improvement store for products specifically designed to clean dry, hard brushes.

Cleaning Alkyd Paint from Brushes

Hoping to use old-fashioned soap and water to get the paint out? Sorry, alkyd paint comes out only with solvent. To keep from making a mess in your sink, use this three-can method instead. Working in a garage or outdoor area is best, but anywhere is fine as long as you protect the area and make sure you have proper ventilation.

Before you begin, put on your gloves and goggles, and find a work area that's well ventilated and away from any heat source or open flame. Lay down newspaper or dropcloths to protect your work surface.

1. Use your wire paint comb to rid the brush of excess wet paint, depositing it back into the paint can.

2. Set out the three containers on the newspaper or dropcloth, and fill each one-third or half full with paint thinner.

3. Put all your brushes into the first container. Let them soak for five minutes, and then wiggle them around — up, down, sideways, and around — to work out the paint.

4. Lay down several layers of paper towels on top of some newspaper to protect the surface where you're working. Remove the brushes from the bath, and place them on the paper towels. Use gentle pressure to press the bristles into the paper towels, blotting off the thinner.

5. Repeat Steps 3 and 4, putting the brushes in the second container of paint thinner.

6. Put the brushes into the third container, and let them soak for three minutes. Wiggle them once or twice. The liquid should be clean.

7. Create a place for the brushes to dry by lining a large cardboard box with a large garbage bag.

8. Remove the brushes from their last bath and, using your gloved hand, squeeze the excess paint thinner back into the third container. Blot the brushes on clean paper towels. No paint should appear on the paper towels, all having been removed from the brushes.

9. Take the brushes to your drying station. Place your hands inside the large cardboard box to contain the spatter, and slap the metal heel of the brush handle against the heel of your hand repeatedly until no liquid is left. Dry with paper towels.

10. Place the brush's original cover back on it, and hang the brush on pegboard or lay it on a flat surface in your storage area to keep it in the best condition. Make sure the bristles aren't bent.

11. Pour all the paint thinner into a single can. Replace the lid, cover it with a rag, and tap the lid back on tightly with a rubber mallet. Contact your local waste disposal service.

Cleaning Latex Paint from Roller Covers and Cages

If you don't plan to reuse your roller cover, simply place it inside a plastic grocery bag, pull it off the metal roller cage, and toss the bag and roller cover in the trash. Clean the roller cage, and you're done! If your philosophy is "waste not, want not," you can clean both items and use them again. All you need is soap and water to rid rolling equipment of latex paint. Just make sure your roller cover has a plastic core that will stand up to water.

1. Put on rubber gloves to keep your hands clean. Use the curved side of your 5-in-1 tool to scrape off any excess paint from the roller cover into the paint container. You may need to scrape for a minute or two to work out as much paint as possible.

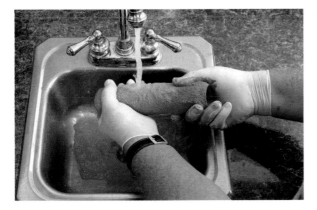

2. Working over your paint tray, pull the roller cover off the cage; set the cage aside for now. Rinse the cover under warm running water, massaging it from top to bottom with either your 5-in-1 tool or your hands until the water runs clear.

3. Fill the sink with warm water and mild liquid soap. Wash the cover in the sudsy water, rubbing it with your hands to work the soapy water well into the fibers.

4. Drain the sink, and then rinse the roller cover until the water runs clean. Squeeze out excess water with your hands by encircling the roller cover with your fingers and thumb and sliding your hand in one direction. It may take several passes to get all the water out.

5. Stand the roller cover on its end atop some newspapers to dry. When dry, store it on a shelf on its end.

6. Wash the metal roller cage in the sink with mild liquid soap. Use a wire brush to work off any dried paint that isn't released by soap and some elbow grease. Rinse the cage, pat it dry with a paper towel, and store it.

To get the most water out of a wet roller cover, place the roller cover on the clean cage, take it outside, and spin the roller as fast as you can to expel the water from the roller.

Cleaning Alkyd Paint from Roller Covers and Cages

Alkyd paint doesn't come off with soap and water. You need to use paint thinner and the three-can method instead. Lambswool roller covers are probably worth saving, but if you've worked with alkyd paint, consider tossing the synthetic kind. Just slip a plastic grocery bag over the cover, slide it off the metal cage, and toss it in the trash. If you want to clean and reuse your rolling equipment, this project's for you.

1. Put on latex gloves and goggles, and find a work area that's well ventilated and away from any heat source or open flame. Lay down newspaper or dropcloths to protect your work surface.

2. Fill three containers with enough paint thinner or mineral spirits to cover a roller cover laid flat.

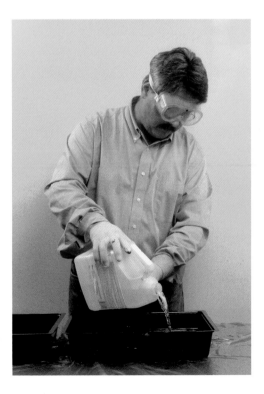

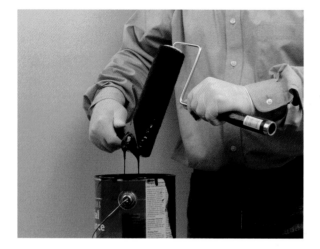

3. Use the curved edge of your 5-in-1 tool to scrape paint from the roller cover back into the paint container or can. You may need to scrape for a minute or two to work out as much paint as possible.

4. Working over your paint tray, slip the roller cover off the cage. Lay it in one of the containers of paint thinner, and set the cage aside. Let the cover soak for five minutes, wiggling it around periodically to loosen the paint.

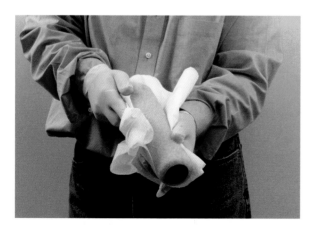

5. Remove the cover from the first container, scrape off excess liquid with the curved side of a 5-in-1 tool, and then wipe off the cover with paper towels. (Wiping at this stage helps to remove some of the diluted paint and/or mineral spirits.)

6. Lay the cover in the second container of paint thinner. Let it soak for three minutes, and then wiggle it around to remove more paint.

7. Repeat Step 5.

8. Put the cover into the third container of paint thinner. Let it soak for two minutes, and then wiggle it around.

9. Repeat Step 5, and then stand the roller cover on its end atop a stack of paper towels to dry. (If you stand the cover on newspaper, you could reactivate the ink in the paper and ruin your cover.)

10. Let the roller cage sit in the first container of paint thinner for two minutes. Remove it and wipe it with paper towels to remove loose paint.

11. Repeat Step 10, let the roller cage dry completely, and store it.

Fixing problems after the fact

No matter how much you try to focus on your painting and the job at hand, some problems reveal themselves only after the paint dries and you think the project's finished. The most common problems you find afterward are listed here. Although the problems themselves are different, the fix is essentially the same: Prep the surface (see Chapters 2 and 3) and apply another coat of paint using the same roller or brush that you used the first time around (see Chapter 4).

- ✔ **Uneven coverage:** White specks in the painted surface are primer or undercoat showing through and an indication that you need another coat of paint. Dark splotches are an indication that you didn't stir the paint thoroughly in the can before using it.

- ✔ **Uneven paint finish:** The problem may just be the lighting in the room. Adjust the light in that particular area by changing the direction of the light, changing the bulb, getting a new fixture, or adjusting window coverings and the level of sunlight on the surface. If you still see a mix of finishes, the problem may be that you mixed up your paints, accidentally touching up a matte finish with semi-gloss or vice versa. Use 220-grit sandpaper to sand the uneven area until the paint is dull. Then use a hand vacuum to remove any residue, and repaint the area with the correct paint.

- ✔ **Damaged paint:** Over time, your paint job may suffer scrapes, dings, or even lose its luster thanks to overzealous cleaning. Before you repaint the damaged area, scrape away loose paint using a 5-in-1 tool, sand the area with 220-grit sandpaper, and wipe or vacuum away any residue.

- ✔ **Drips:** Drips are likely the result of overloading your brush or roller and applying too much paint. To erase a dry drip, use 220-grit sandpaper to sand downward over the drip, working in only one direction. You want to sand away only the drip and spare the surrounding paint. Wipe or vacuum any residue from the area, and touch up the paint using a trim brush and a light stroke.

Cleaning paint spills and spatters

The best advice for cleaning up spills and spatters is to paint carefully and clean up as you go. If you find paint on your skin, clothes, or elsewhere, this list tells you how to remove it:

- ✔ **Cleaning paint from your skin:** Latex paints come off with soap and water. Use a soft nylon brush and gentle soap — both should be made for use on skin — and rinse with warm water. Don't use thinner or other chemicals — they're toxic and can make you sick. For hard-to-remove substances, such as alkyd or oil-based paints, pick up specialized skin cleaner from your home improvement store (auto parts stores sell it, too).

- ✔ **Cleaning paint from clothes:** Most latex paint washes out with warm water and detergent. Pretreat the stained area with a solution of detergent and water. Wash on the longest cycle possible. Repeat as needed. Never dry clothes that have stains because the heat sets the stain. For alkyd paint, dab some paint thinner on the spot and rinse well in water. Wash separately.

- ✔ **Cleaning paint from carpet:** Use a damp, not wet, sponge and gently blot to lift latex paint. You may have to repeat this step several times. You can also find commercial products for cleaning dry latex paint at your hardware store. Clean alkyd paint drips immediately — don't let them dry. Repeatedly dab a clean rag dipped in mineral spirits on the paint spot. It takes time to get all the paint out, but it should clean up. If the paint dries, you can only scrape the drip gently and hope that you'll remove some of the paint.

Storing Paint

Stuff You Need to Know

Toolbox:
- Newspaper
- Leftover paint
- Paintbrush
- Small empty paint cans
- Paint strainer or cheesecloth
- Permanent marker
- Towel or rag
- Rubber mallet

Time Needed:
Less than an hour

Properly saved paint can last up to three years, so you should definitely save your leftover paint for touch ups. The trick is to minimize the air — the enemy of paint — inside the can. For example, if you finish your project with about a quart of paint left and you store it in the gallon-sized container that it came in, all the excess air in the can will dry out the paint. Buy extra gallon- and quart-sized cans to hold your leftovers. Empty paint cans cost only a dollar or two and are well worth it.

1. Cover your workspace in newspaper, and then pour the leftover paint from roller trays and containers into the original paint can (so that it's easier to pour into the strainer after all the paint has been collected). Use a paintbrush to sweep out all excess paint that may have collected on the sides and bottom of the containers, getting as much paint as possible back into the original can.

2. Set up the new can with a strainer on top. Strain all the debris that may have been left behind by brushes and rollers by pouring the paint into the new can through a strainer. Let the strained paint run into the smallest can that will hold it all.

3. Put a dot of paint on the lid, and use a permanent marker to write all the paint information on the can. Include the manufacturer, paint name, type of finish, date of purchase, and place of purchase.

4. Place the lid on the can, cover it with a towel or rag, and tap it shut using a rubber mallet to keep from distorting the lid. Tap only around the perimeter of the lid, *not* in the center (that will bend the lid and hinder its ability to seal correctly). If you don't have a mallet, place a piece of wood over the lid and use your hammer to tap the wood.

5. Store the paint in a cool, dry place.

You should always store paint away from heat, which means away from water heaters, clothes dryers, dishwashers, direct sunlight, and anything that may raise the ambient temperature or create a spark. If you wish to dispose of paint or other toxic chemicals, you must contact your local waste disposal site. Paint is toxic to plants, pets, and people. Treat it as hazardous waste and don't pour it down a drain or dispose of it in a landfill.

Recording paint information on the can is important because if you need to purchase more paint or if there's a problem with the paint, the paint store will have all the information needed to either make more or fix the problem.

Part II
Painting Walls
Like a Pro

The 5th Wave — By Rich Tennant

"I'm not sure I should continue rag rolling the walls in here. I don't think I'm doing it right, and Rags is getting tired, too."

In this part . . .

You can probably tell at a glance whether a paint job was done by a child or an adult. But is it so easy to tell whether a room was painted by a professional or an amateur? It depends on how much know-how that amateur has. In this part, we give you what you need to up your game to the professional level.

Faux finishes and impressive effects take center stage in this part. Leaf through the pages to see what you can achieve with paint, glaze, the proper tools, and the two things no painter can do without: patience and perseverance. Follow the photos and read through the step-by-step instructions to make these fun decorative techniques come to life in your own home.

Chapter 5

Faux Finishes with Shapes and Patterns

Faux finishes (pronounced *foh,* French for *false*) are paint techniques that make a painted wall look old when it's new, rough when it's smooth, or like some other material — such as leather or silk — when it's not. By adding dimension and drama to otherwise plain surfaces, they give you lots of decorative bang for the buck just for the price of the paint and your time.

A common mistake that amateur painters make on faux finishes is banding the corners. Avoid this mistake by working on two opposing — not adjacent — walls on the first day of your weekend project. On the second day, mask off the walls you did the previous day with *delicate stick tape.* If you do only two opposing walls each day, you can mask off the opposite walls and work up to the tape. This trick helps you avoid an odd line around the room and keep corners consistent without affecting the look of walls that are next to each other.

Measure twice, paint once

Shapes and patterns may give the impression that they're random. But, in fact, you have to measure, level, and figure if you want to do several of the designs in this chapter. If you paint vertical stripes on the wall without penciling in the stripes and without using a plumb line, you quickly realize that two walls don't always meet at a precise 90-degree angle.

Create a *plumb line* by hanging a weighted string on a nail at the top of a wall — use a string that reaches from the ceiling almost to the floor. When you're painting stripes, measure them from this exact vertical line. Follow these steps to mark off the placement of your first stripe:

1. **Put a yardstick right on top of the plumb line and measure off where the first stripe will start.**

2. **Mark the spot by making a small mark with your pencil.**

3. **Move the yardstick to another spot on the plumb line, and make another pencil mark.**

4. **Repeat until you have enough pencil marks to draw a straight line from the ceiling to the floor.**

5. **Follow all the steps again to mark off the other side of your first stripe.**

Use these steps to measure and pencil in each stripe along one wall. Then rehang the plumb line on another wall and start all over again. For best results, do some calculating ahead of time so that you don't run out of space for the square or stripe you want to end up with.

Putting on Vertical Stripes

Stuff You Need to Know

Toolbox:

- Tools and materials for prep (see Chapter 2)
- Tools and materials for base coat (see Chapter 4)
- Satin finish latex paint for base coat
- Tape measure
- Colored pencil
- 4-foot level
- 2-inch blue painter's tape
- Satin finish latex paint for stripes
- Mini-roller
- Roller tray and liner
- Sponge
- Paint guard
- 2-inch angled sash brush

Time Needed:
About a day

Stripes can be horizontal or vertical, thin or thick, simple one color or trickier two (or more) colors, precisely or imprecisely edged. You also can alternate the widths of your lines or make the spacing consistent. Whether you use semi-gloss and flat sheens of the same color or sharply contrasting colors, stripes are lively and work well for dining rooms, hallways, and powder rooms. Generally, your base color should be lighter than your stripe or stripes.

1. Prep the room according to the instructions in Chapter 2. Paint on the base color (see Chapter 4) and let it dry for at least 4 hours. You can paint over a pre-existing base coat as long as it's eggshell, satin, or semi-gloss.

2. Determine the width of the stripes. Measure each wall with a tape measure and divide the length of your wall by the width of your stripe to figure out how many stripes you'll have. Plan out the stripe pattern so that you don't end up with any partial stripes in awkward places. ***Example:*** If your wall is 10 feet wide and you want your stripes to be 6 inches wide, you can place 20 stripes on the wall. (Convert 10 feet to 120 inches, and then 120 inches ÷ 6 inches = 20.)

3. Pace off horizontal spacing between stripes. Start at eye level in the most inconspicuous spot (at a corner near the door) and measure off the inches according to your plan. Marking every 4 to 5 inches creates a traditional wide stripe. Mark the stripe spacing with a colored pencil that closely matches the stripe paint.

4. Repeat Step 3 both above and below your first set of marks (like at the ceiling and at baseboard level) so that you have three marks for each line.

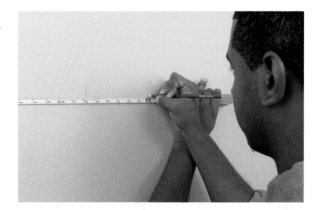

5. Use a level to draw a vertical line down from each mark at the ceiling toward the floor, using your colored pencil. Use light pressure to make marks, and use all the marks as guidelines.

6. Mask off every other stripe with blue painter's tape. *Burnish* the tape by running a plastic putty knife or credit card over it in both directions to make sure the tape is pressed tightly against the wall and the paint won't bleed under it.

7. Mark the stripes that you're *not* going to paint with pieces of tape. You may want to put Xs on them to indicate that you don't paint those stripes.

8. Paint the stripes onto the wall with your mini-roller. Roll over the tape to prevent working it off the wall and creating seepage.

9. Pull the tape off the wall as soon as possible after completing each stripe. Pull off the tape as you work around the room. If you peel off the tape and notice seepage and bleeding, clean off the paint with a damp sponge. If it's too late, you'll have to repaint the base color stripes. Use a paint guard and 2-inch angled sash brush to touch up, or wait until the other stripes are dry before masking the areas off and touching up.

Using metric measurements is a lot easier than using inches (and fractions!) when you're spacing out your stripes. You don't have to wear out your brain trying to interpret what those little lines mean or keep a lot of strange numbers in your head long enough to write them down. In the long run, you'll make fewer mistakes.

If you've ever seen professional painters on decorating shows scratching their heads in confusion as they try to figure out a two-tone pattern, you know the danger of skipping Step 7! Don't do it! Any extra time you spend marking sections to paint is worthwhile because you end up making fewer mistakes in the long run.

Putting on Horizontal Stripes

Stuff You Need to Know

Toolbox:
- Tools and materials for prep (see Chapter 2)
- Tools and materials for base coat (see Chapter 4)
- Satin finish latex paint in dark, medium, and light shades of the same color
- Tape measure
- 4-foot level (or a laser level if you have one)
- Pencil
- 2-inch blue painter's tape
- Utility knife
- Roller cover
- Roller cage
- Roller tray and liner
- 2-inch angled sash brush
- Artist's brush

Time Needed:
About a day

For a contemporary look, create three equal horizontal bands of graduated color with the darkest color on the bottom. The effect, created by Miami designer Alfredo Brito, makes low-ceiling rooms look less squatty. From a paint strip, pick a dark, medium, and light color. Grays, browns, and neutralized colors work best.

1. Prep the room according to Chapter 2, and then paint the wall the light base color. Let it dry for at least 4 hours. (See Chapter 4 if you need more information on painting a base coat.)

2. Measure the height of your wall with a tape measure and divide it into three sections (top, middle, and bottom). Mark off the three sections using a level and a pencil. Follow these lines horizontally around the room.

3. Use painter's tape to prep the middle of your three sections. Mask off the top section by placing the tape just above the pencil line. Mask off the bottom section by placing the tape just below the pencil line.

4. To prevent seeping paint under the tape, use a horizontal motion to score the top of the tape that's above the bottom section with a utility knife.

5. Use your roller to paint the middle strip with the medium paint color. Let it dry for 4 hours, and then remove the tape.

6. Mask off the middle section by placing tape on top of the bottom edge of the middle section. You don't want any space between the middle and bottom sections. You don't need to score this tape line.

7. Use your roller to apply the dark color all the way to the floor (painting over any baseboards; see Chapter 9 for trim painting tips).

8. Remove the tape.

If you remove the tape and you notice that the line isn't straight, you can use an artist's brush and the appropriate paint color to clean up the edges.

If you're using this technique on the entire room, mark all the walls with the carpenter's level (or laser level) and a pencil first. Mask off the middle stripe all the way around the room, paint all the middle stripes, and let them dry. Use a 2-inch angled sash brush to cut in corners. Mask for the bottom sections all the way around the room, and paint all the bottom stripes at the same time.

Decorating with Stencils

You can use stencils to create allover, random, or discrete patterns and decorative borders horizontally at the ceiling or chair rail level of a wall or vertically on a wall. This project guides you through the application of a horizontally aligned stencil using two colors.

Precut stencils in every architectural and decorative style are widely available at arts and crafts, home improvement, and paint stores. For a unique style statement, make your own stencils by cutting out a design with a hobby knife from a sheet of Mylar plastic. For unexpected flair, layer two or more stencils to create a custom design. (Simply proceed around the room with one stencil, let the paint dry for at least an hour, and then go back around applying paint with the other stencil.)

1. Prepare your stencil by cutting away with your utility knife any hanging bits or parts of your precut stencil pattern that aren't perfectly clean.

2. Dust any debris off the stencil with a clean rag.

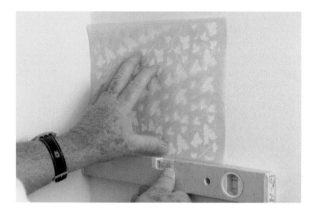

3. Place the top of the stencil at the height you want it on your wall in an inconspicuous corner of the room. Place your level along the bottom of the stencil, and make necessary adjustments for level.

4. Tape the stencil in place with a small piece of blue tape on each of the four corners.

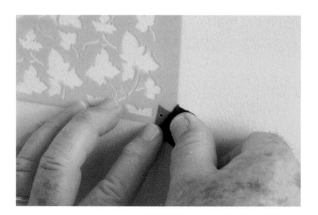

5. Find one of the stencil's four registration points (found in the four corners), and lift one corner of the stencil away from the wall. Place a small piece of blue painter's tape on the wall under the stencil at the registration point. Put the corner back down.

6. Use a pencil to mark the registration hole on the blue tape. Repeat this process with the other three registration points on the stencil.

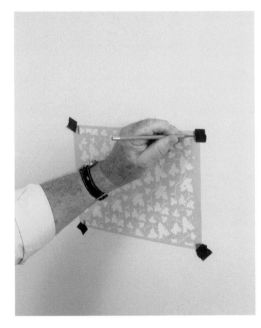

7. Remove the stencil from the wall and place it immediately to the right of its previous placement, aligning the left registration points with the right ones that you marked with blue tape in Steps 5 and 6. Tape the stencil in place.

8. Lift one of the right two corners of the stencil, place a piece of blue tape under the registration point, put the corner back down, and mark the registration point on the tape with a pencil. Repeat with the other right corner.

9. Repeat Steps 7 and 8 all the way around the room. The last stencil probably won't be a complete pattern, which is why you should always start and end in an inconspicuous corner.

10. Put on your latex gloves, and prepare your paint by shaking or stirring up the paint or paints you're using with your stencil. Pour some of each paint onto a plastic plate.

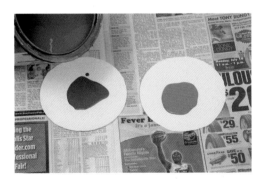

11. In a well-ventilated area, lay down newspaper and place the stencil facedown on top. Spray adhesive on the back of the stencil and let it set until tacky to the touch.

12. Place the stencil on the wall, aligning the four registration points on the stencil with the points on the blue tape, and press it into place. To make sure the stencil doesn't move around on the wall, you may want to tack each corner with a bit of blue tape.

13. Load a brush with paint by gently dipping the tips of the brush in the paint.

14. Blot off excess paint by tapping the bristle tips on a paper towel in a straight, vertical motion. The brush is ready to go when the bristles look almost dry.

15. Starting at the outer perimeters of the stencil, lightly pounce color onto the wall by quickly touching the bristles to the wall and pulling the brush straight away. Stencil the design by working from the outside of the stencil to the inside.

16. Use the same pouncing action and clean brushes to apply a second highlight or lowlight color to the stenciled design as desired.

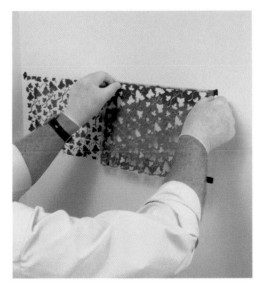

17. To reposition the stencil farther along the wall, lift the stencil off the wall with one clean motion, and align the registration points with the ones you marked on blue tape on the wall. You don't need to reapply adhesive as you move around the room.

Note: As you work your way around the room or surface, clean the paint off the stencil periodically to prevent bleeding and seepage. Lay the stencil on a flat, protected surface, and use a damp paper towel to wipe off excess paint.

The pouncing motion is done perpendicular to the wall surface. Don't stroke your brush from side to side or up and down or you'll end up working the paint under the stencil and losing the definition of the design.

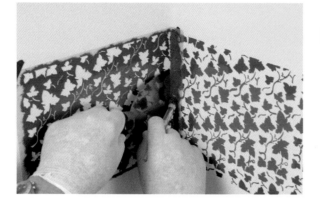

18. To stencil in a corner, use gentle pressure to hold the stencil in place, and apply paint in the same pouncing manner. Be careful not to use so much pressure that you bend the stencil and distort the design. If you're having trouble, use a drywall spackle knife to hold the stencil in place; line up the stencil's registration points and then gently press the knife (vertically) straight into the corner.

19. After you stencil your design all around the room or space that you're working in, go back and fill in blank spots and gaps with an artist's small liner brush and very little paint. Blot excess paint on a paper towel, and make sure that the brush is almost dry before you touch up the stencil.

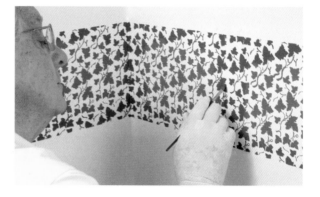

If your design involves using a second overlay stencil, complete one wall or section before going back over the design with the overlay stencil. Match up the registration marks on the overlay, and repeat the steps in this project.

Some stencils look best if the paint coverage has variation whereas others look better if the coverage is even and complete. Experiment first on a piece of poster board to find the look you like. For uneven coverage, vary the angle of the brush. For even coverage, go over the stencil pattern a second time.

Creating Cloudy Skies

Stuff You Need to Know

Toolbox:

- Pencil and paper to sketch clouds
- Tools and materials for prep (see Chapter 2)
- Tools and materials for base coat (see Chapter 4)
- Satin finish latex paint in sky blue for base coat
- Three buckets
- Glaze
- Satin finish latex paint in white for clouds
- Satin finish latex paint in purple-blue for cloud lowlights
- Satin finish latex paint in pale pink for cloud highlights
- Stir sticks
- Four 2-inch flat sash brushes
- Clean rags
- Large sheepskin pad

Time Needed:
About a weekend, including overnight dry time

Big fluffy clouds are easier to create with paint than you may think. Use them on bathroom ceilings and children's rooms or anywhere else you want a bit of peaceful whimsy. A great thing about clouds is that they don't have to cover every surface — paint them above a chair rail, on the top third of each wall, or on only one focal wall or the ceiling.

The key to pretty, realistic clouds is layering glazes in lighter and darker blues, white, and even a little pink. Because you work with a number of paint colors and different tools, take your sky and clouds on a trial run by painting them on poster boards.

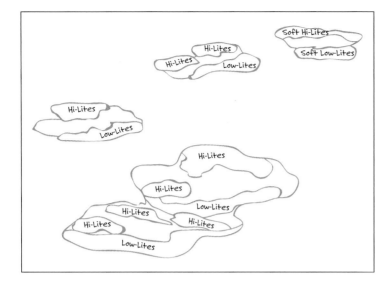

1. Sketch a scaled-down version of your fluffy clouds on a piece of paper. (One sheet of 8½-x-11-inch paper neatly accommodates a plan for one 8-x-10-foot wall.) Cloud formations should overlap and vary in length, height, and fluffiness. For inspiration, look at some of your own photographs as well as photography books or Web sites.

2. Prep the room according to instructions in Chapter 2, and paint on the sky blue base color (see Chapter 4 for info on painting a base coat). Let the base coat dry at least 4 hours to overnight. Leave up any tape or masking.

3. Mix three glazes in the buckets: one for the white clouds, one for the cloud lowlights, and one for the cloud highlights. Check the glaze manufacturer's instructions for paint-to-glaze-to-water ratios. Increase the amount of glaze for greater translucency. Stir each glaze mixture thoroughly with a stir stick.

4. Float your first cloud by using a 2-inch flat sash brush to paint a long, irregular streak of white glaze at the visual center of your focal wall.

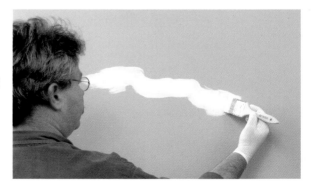

5. Tap the streak gently with the large sheep-skin pad to remove excess paint and fluff out the cloud. Take off more paint toward the edges of the cloud so that it appears to gradually blend into the blue sky.

6. Refer to your sketch for the placement of your next cloud, and repeat Steps 4 and 5, applying paint and blending it with the sheepskin. Repeat for all the other clouds on the wall.

7. To make the clouds more realistic and dramatic, use the purple-blue glaze toward the upper region of your sky and overlapping some of the clouds. Apply wavy strokes of purple-blue glaze with a 2-inch flat sash brush.

8. Dampen a clean rag, wring it out well, and wad it up. Use the rag to dab the purple-blue glaze, blending it into the white clouds and the blue sky at the edges.

9. Use a 2-inch flat sash brush to add streaks of pink glaze highlights to the crests of the clouds.

10. With the sheepskin pad, tap and pounce the pink glaze to blend it in with the surrounding colors.

Cloud painting kits are widely available at home improvement, paint supply, and craft stores. They come with the tools needed for the job, and some even include paints or at the very least recommendations of specific paint colors.

If a cloud or two looks too heavy after the glaze dries, use a small sponge to pounce on sky blue glaze. Mix the glaze in a small container with a ratio of ½ cup glaze to ½ cup paint.

Color Blocking

If you can put tape on a wall, you can color block. This super-simple technique is great for creating a high-impact wall (but resist the temptation to overdo it by using the technique on every wall in a room), and it's a great way to draw eyes to framed photos or artwork.

Make sure you *burnish* the painter's tape, which means that you run a plastic putty knife or a credit card over it in both directions. If you don't get a tight seal from your tape, the paint is likely to bleed and you lose the sharp lines you're aiming for.

1. Prepare the room and walls according to the instructions in Chapter 2. Cut in and roll on your base coat (see Chapter 4 if you need help painting a base coat). Apply a second coat, if necessary, and allow the base coat to dry completely, preferably overnight.

2. After you settle on the design you want, begin measuring off the squares. Use the level to make sure your lines are straight, and mark the design with a pencil along the yardstick.

TIP

Use a computer word processing program to experiment with color combinations and color-block arrangements. Microsoft Word has an "AutoShapes" function that allows you to easily create boxes, fill them with color, move them around, and change their dimensions.

3. Tape along the outside edges of your pencil marks.

4. Select one of your darker, coordinating paint colors. Pour the paint into the tray and prepare your smooth-surface paint roller by loading it with paint.

5. Use the roller to apply paint inside the tape lines for every shape that you want to paint this color. If you're using another darker, coordinating paint color, leave some of the shapes unpainted for now.

6. Repeat Step 3 for the blocks that you want in the second color.

7. Pour your second paint color into a tray and paint all the blocks you've taped off.

8. If you want to use a third color, repeat Steps 3 and 7 with the third color.

9. Let paint dry 4 to 6 hours, and then remove the tape.

Crafting a Tone-on-Tone Checkerboard

Stuff You Need to Know

Toolbox:

- Tools and materials for prep (see Chapter 2)
- Tools and materials for base coat (see Chapter 4)
- Eggshell finish latex paint for base coat
- Yardstick
- Colored pencil
- Small level
- 2-inch blue painter's tape
- Latex gloves
- Stir sticks
- Semi-gloss finish latex paint (same color as eggshell finish) for top coat
- Roller tray and liner
- Mini-roller

Time Needed:

About a weekend

A pattern of matte and semi-gloss paint squares gives a wall a cool, contemporary look that's high-impact without taking over the room. You use one color in two finishes to paint a clean, tone-on-tone checkerboard pattern.

1. Prep the room according to the instructions in Chapter 2, and paint on the eggshell finish base coat (see Chapter 4 for more on painting a base coat). Let the base coat dry at least 4 hours to overnight. Leave up any tape or masking.

2. Measure the length and height of your wall to determine the size squares (or rectangles, if necessary) that will best fit. You want the squares to be at least 12 inches on each side. For example, if your wall is 9 feet tall by 15 feet wide, 18-inch squares fit evenly into the space; this is the size square used in the remainder of this project.

3. Using the yardstick and colored pencil, tick off 18-inch increments across the wall. Use the yardstick and small level side by side to draw straight vertical lines on the wall.

4. Using the yardstick and colored pencil, tick off 18-inch increments from top to bottom along the wall. Use the yardstick and level side by side to draw straight horizontal lines on the wall.

5. Place a piece of blue tape in the center of every other square, alternating in each row so that you mark off a checkerboard pattern. These are the squares that will remain in the eggshell finish.

6. Apply blue painter's tape to the penciled lines on either side of the squares marked in Step 5. Start with the row closest to the ceiling, and tape off alternating squares in every other row. *Burnish* the tape by running a plastic putty knife or credit card over it in both directions to make sure the tape is pressed tightly against the wall and the paint won't bleed under it.

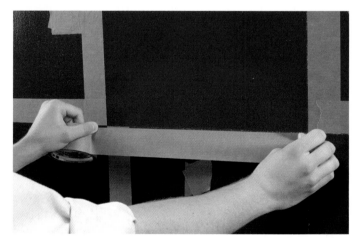

7. Put on latex gloves, and use a stir stick to thoroughly stir the semi-gloss paint. Pour some into a paint tray.

8. Use a mini-roller to paint the untaped squares with semi-gloss paint. *Remember:* You're painting the squares *not* marked with tape in Step 5, and you're painting alternate squares in every other row. Let the paint dry completely before carefully removing the tape.

Disposing of paint and cleanup liquids

Paint is toxic to plants, pets, and people. Treat it as hazardous waste and don't pour it down a drain or dispose of it in a landfill. If you do, it may eventually leach into and contaminate the groundwater. Here are some ways that you can be green:

✔ **To clean brushes and rollers:** Use your handy 5-in-1 tool to scrape off all excess paint from rollers and brushes into paint cans. Or you can use a spinner to spin off the excess paint into a container — either a cardboard box or 5-gallon paint bucket lined with a trash bag — and then take the trash to a disposal site for hazardous waste. After you get rid of the excess paint, you can clean your rollers and brushes as normal (see the projects in Chapter 4 that tell you how to clean paint from roller covers and cages for details).

✔ **To dispose of cleanup supplies:** Put all your cleanup liquids into a 5-gallon bucket and store the covered container in a cool, dry place. Collect all your solvent-soaked rags and toss them into a bag. Do the same for all your old paint cans (make sure lids are shut tight). You can then take them to a hazardous waste disposal site or the site your community designates.

Remember: If you don't know your community's policies on disposing of chemicals, contact your local government. (Most towns have a Web site with this info.) Don't forget to ask your homeowners association about disposing of paint — some associations have stringent guidelines.

Harlequin Pattern

A harlequin pattern looks great but can be maddening if you try to apply it to big spaces or around corners. That endeavor requires a level of math and measuring that we can't recommend in good conscience. So we suggest that you use a harlequin pattern instead in a nook or as a backsplash. Or apply it as a border, on one narrow wall, or above a chair rail.

1. Prep the room according to instructions in Chapter 2, and paint on your desired base color (see Chapter 4 for more on painting a base coat). Let the base coat dry at least 4 hours to overnight, and then apply a second coat for good coverage if desired. Leave up any tape or masking.

2. Plot diamonds on the wall in whatever size you want. Diamonds should be about twice as long as they are wide. Use the yardstick and level to ensure that your diamonds line up vertically and horizontally, and mark the points in colored pencil.

3. Using the yardstick and colored pencil, draw diagonal lines connecting the points to create the diamond shapes.

4. Place a piece of blue tape in the center of every diamond in every other row. (If you look at the wall from an angle, it should look like a checkerboard pattern.) These are the squares that will remain in the base coat color.

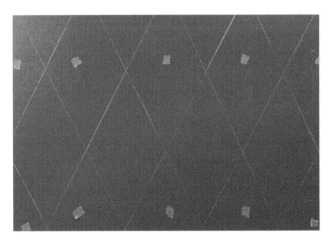

5. Starting with the row closest to the ceiling, apply blue painter's tape to the penciled lines on either side of the diamonds marked in Step 4. Tape off all the diamonds in this row, and *burnish* the tape by running a plastic putty knife or credit card over it in both directions to make sure the tape is pressed tightly against the wall and the paint won't bleed under it.

6. Repeat Step 5 in every other row (the diamonds marked with tape in the center) to the bottom of the wall.

7. Put on gloves, and use a stir stick to stir the second (accent) color of paint thoroughly. Pour some into a paint tray.

8. Using a mini-roller, apply the accent paint to the untaped diamonds.

9. Let the paint dry completely (about 4 to 6 hours) before carefully removing the tape. Let the paint dry overnight.

Turn a hair dryer on the lowest setting and wave it over the tape before you remove it to loosen the adhesive and to help make sure that the paint doesn't come up with the tape.

If the points of your diamonds don't quite match up, use a small square or circular stamp to apply a third color at the joints. This accent easily covers the rough joints without detracting from the design.

Chapter 6

Faux Finishes Using Glaze

Tasks performed in this chapter

✔ Colorwashing

✔ Glazed wall treatment

✔ Basic dragging

✔ Dragging on wavy lines

✔ Faux leather wall finish

✔ Ragging on

✔ Ragging off

✔ Sponging on

✔ Sponging off

✔ Chambray brush effect

✔ Bagging

✔ Frottage

Faux finishes, like the ones in this chapter, generally call for a base coat and one or more glaze coats or other specialized pearl, opal, metallic, or sandy-texture paints. Think of the *base coat* as the fresh paint you just put on your walls — the final coat when you don't plan any special wall treatments. When you're tackling the special treatments in this chapter, the base coat serves as the undercoat for glaze. But remember that the base coat contributes color to the overall effect of the faux finish, so you want to select a base coat color that's compatible with your color scheme. You can apply the base coat anywhere from 4 hours, absolute minimum, to 7 days before you apply the glaze. But don't wait too long to glaze or you'll need to clean your walls (and then wait for them to dry) before you faux.

You have two choices in selecting paint for a base coat. The first is to choose any latex satin or semi-gloss paint. That gives you an opportunity to create your own color palette and make sure it coordinates with the furnishings in your home. The other option is to go to the paint store and purchase products sold exclusively as base coats and coordinating glazes. These products come in various colors. Look for the informative pamphlets; they have color photos showing how each finish will look if you use a different glaze or technique. And they tell you what tools you need.

If you want to create your own palette, just make sure that you have latex satin or semi-gloss paint for the base. (Your walls don't have to be freshly painted, but make sure you wash them thoroughly before you get started.) The paint store or home improvement center will tint a transparent glaze to your specifications; don't worry about pigmentation — the store takes care of that too.

If you're adventurous enough to tint your own glaze, read the manufacturer's instructions first. Most manufacturers say to use one quart of your color with a gallon of glaze, but directions may vary from brand to brand. And buy quality glaze. It pays off in ease of use and the pattern and texture of the finished product.

Always use a paint that has some sheen as a base coat. Eggshell will work, but satin or semi-gloss interior latex paint is preferred. Matte paint won't work — it's porous and dull.

After you put down the base coat and let it dry, you're ready to apply the glaze coat. Glazes are either added or taken away with one of these two basic techniques:

✔ **Positive/additive:** Techniques that call for applying glaze to select areas over the base coat are called *positive* or *additive techniques* because glaze is added only where you want it. Additive techniques allow most of the base coat to show through.

✔ **Negative/subtractive:** Techniques that call for removing select areas of an allover glaze applied over a base coat are called *negative* or *subtractive techniques* because portions of the glaze are lifted off. Negative techniques cover most of the base coat and therefore emphasize the glaze color.

Creating faux finishes can be a lot of fun. To make sure that your faux finish experiences are good ones, experiment! Follow these tips:

✔ Always practice on cardboard or poster board first to test the technique and your color choices. Try out various color combinations, using hues that coordinate with your furnishings. The poster board gives you a chance to experiment with the amount of glaze to use and how to use different tools.

  Use glaze in a combination of colors and reverse the order in which they're applied to find out which one you like most. Try putting a medium glaze on the base color, and then adding a lighter glaze. Glaze another section that has the medium glaze on top.

✔ Vary the way in which you hold equipment. For instance, change the angle of a brush or use each side of a sea sponge to give glaze different effects. Pick the one you prefer before starting the project.

✔ Don't limit yourself to tools just for faux painting. Whisk brooms, dust mops, squeegees, and ordinary sponges (all new, naturally) create different looks.

✔ For more complex finishes, layer additive and subtractive techniques, using different glaze colors for each step.

✔ Have two (or more) sets of finishing tools — one for working with the first section (or couple of sections) and another one for subsequent sections. Your sponges, rags, and other tools for fauxing can become too saturated with paint to maintain the integrity of your desired effect. Clean off oversaturated brushes with damp rags and sponges, or give them a quick rinse and spin dry for use on other areas.

✔ After you finish your project, brush on a clear sealant, such as polyurethane or a protective coating put out by the manufacturer. Seal the finish especially when it's in a high traffic area or to protect flat surfaces on desks, tables, and dressers.

When you're applying glaze, speed — not accuracy — is the issue. Although you (usually) don't have to thoroughly cover an area with paint or leave clean edges, you do need to work with glaze while it's wet. Work with a partner when you have a lot to do, the surface is large, or the day is hot and dry (glaze dries quicker on these days).

To help you work quickly, section your wall off mentally before you start glazing. Work in a 4-by-4-foot space, staring an adjacent section while the glaze is still wet. After you glaze one section of the wall, finish it with your sponge (or other finishing tool) almost to the edge, leaving a wet border. Then, without putting more glaze on the border, glaze another complete section. When it's wet, go back to the border and sponge it, working your way across the new section. But stop in time to leave another wet border on the edges, and then start sponging again. Repeat glazing and finishing, section by section, until you complete the wall.

Colorwashing

Stuff You Need to Know

Toolbox:

- ✔ Tools and materials for prep (see Chapter 2)
- ✔ Tools and materials for base coat (see Chapter 4)
- ✔ Eggshell or satin finish latex paint for base coat
- ✔ Glaze
- ✔ Latex paint in medium and dark shades for glaze
- ✔ Two buckets or small paint containers
- ✔ Stir sticks
- ✔ Two 3-inch flat sash brushes
- ✔ Clean terry cloth towels
- ✔ Clean rags
- ✔ Small chip brush

Time Needed:

About a day plus 4 hours of dry time

Colorwashing creates glowing color and great depth that calls to mind the ambiance of a country villa. It's a perfect visual disguise for uneven walls, but it looks great on smooth ones, too. Colorwashing calls for using two strongly related glaze colors — one medium and the other a deep variation — over a neutral base coat to create a distressed, time worn, old-world finish. Any neutral or neutralized color works well as a base coat. You can stay within the color family by using the lightest value of your glaze color palette. Or you can use white.

To create the look, use a big brush to apply and blend out the deep color over your medium midground hue. Change the position of your wrist and arm often, switch directions frequently, and stand back to take a look after you complete a section. You can fix what doesn't look quite right as long as you work quickly, before the glaze dries. Practice this technique on a piece of poster board first to see how subtle or dramatic you want your finished wall to look.

1. Prep the room according to the instructions in Chapter 2. Cut in and roll on a base coat (see Chapter 4 for instructions on applying a solid coat of paint). Let dry at least 4 hours to overnight. (You can color-wash over an existing base coat as long as it isn't matte — it has to have some sheen.)

2. According to the manufacturers' instructions, combine glaze with the light and dark paints in two separate buckets or paint containers. Stir thoroughly with stir sticks

3. Use a 3-inch flat sash brush to stroke on the first glaze from your paint container in an "X" starting near the ceiling.

4. Use your other 3-inch flat sash brush to stroke on a second "X" with the second glaze next to the first "X". You're making a checkerboard pattern, slightly overlapping the two glaze colors. Be careful not to have too much paint on your brush — you don't want to create a blob effect on the wall. Working in a 3-by-3-foot section at a time is easiest.

5. After completing each 3-by-3-foot section, take a terry cloth towel and blot over the top of the X's in order to soften the look. Stand back and take a look after you complete a section. Does the brushwork look random? If not, you can "erase" an area with a damp cloth and rework. Does it look too definite? Then blot over some brush lines with a soft, dry rag.

For foolproof colors, pick two variations of a shade from a paint strip. Many strips have three to five tints (white has been added) or tones (black has been added). Make sure that the values (the degree of light versus dark) are distinct so that the effect is satisfactory to you. The farther apart the colors are in tonal value, the more dramatic the effect. You can also create a simplified colorwash by dabbing and brushing only one shade of glaze over a white or neutral background.

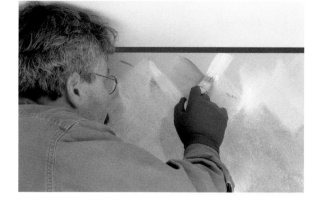

6. Take a small chip brush with some glaze on it and push the glaze into any voids near the ceiling.

7. Move down the wall to the next 3-by-3-foot section and repeat Steps 5 and 6. Always work from a dry undone area back to a wet area.

8. Use a terry cloth towel to blend the sections together as you complete them. You can use your small chip brush to push glaze into the base of the wall and corners.

9. Continue working until you finish the wall, and then go around the room.

Glazed Wall Treatment

Stuff You Need to Know

Toolbox:

- ✔ Tools and materials for prep (see Chapter 2)
- ✔ Tools and materials for base coat (see Chapter 4)
- ✔ Eggshell finish latex paint for base coat
- ✔ Two buckets
- ✔ Latex glaze (tinted)
- ✔ 2-inch flat sash brush
- ✔ Clean rags

Time needed:
About a day plus overnight dry time

This wall finish is an easy way to give a casual and relaxed feeling to a room. You don't have to gather many materials, and the project can be done in one or more layers. Start this project by examining your base color. You can glaze over what's already on your wall, or choose a base color in an eggshell finish to ensure the easiest and best results. Choose a glaze color that's a darker shade than your base color. Ask the retailer to tint it for you.

1. Prepare the room and walls, and tape off windows, doors, and trim (check out Chapter 2 for preparation guidance). Cut in and roll on a base coat (see Chapter 4 for base coat how-to information), and allow it to dry before applying the glaze. If you plan to glaze your existing wall color, proceed to Step 2.

2. Fill one bucket with glaze (check out the manufacturer's instructions for quantities), and fill the other bucket half full with water.

3. Dip the 2-inch flat sash brush into the glaze, and cut in at the upper corner and the ceiling.

4. Dip a damp rag into the glaze and apply it to the wall next to the area you glazed in Step 3. Begin wiping in a small circular or squiggly motion. Blend into the corner and work the glaze out (horizontally) and down (vertically) from the corner until you have no glaze left on the rag. Working in 3-by-3-foot areas is easiest.

5. Start a foot or so away from the wet glaze, and follow Step 4 again, this time blending into the wet area and farther down toward the floor.

6. Continue working wet into wet in blended patches until you finish one wall; continue at the top of the next wall, moving around the room. Be sure to use the brush to cut in at all woodwork.

7. After the walls are completely dry (in general, let it dry overnight), spot touch any light spots by using the same blending technique.

If you're satisfied with the look, you're done. Or you can wait until the glaze is dry to add another layer of a different color. This second layer gives the glaze a deeper shade and has a softer and more blended appearance.

Basic Dragging

Stuff You Need to Know

Toolbox:

- Tools and materials for prep (see Chapter 2)
- Tools and materials for base coat (see Chapter 4)
- Satin finish latex paint for base coat
- Two roller trays and liners (one for the base coat and one for the glaze)
- 4-foot level
- 2-inch blue painter's tape
- Latex gloves
- Bucket
- Glaze
- Satin finish latex paint for glaze
- Stir sticks
- Mini-roller
- Small chip brush
- 3-inch dragging brush, wallpaper brush, or wood graining comb
- Clean rags

Time Needed:
About a weekend

Dragging is a paint technique that involves applying a base coat and a glaze and then dragging over the glaze to subtract some of it and partially reveal the base coat. It can be used to create a number of looks, including strié (from the French word for "striate" or "stripe"), grasscloth, denim, and linen.

Ideally, dragging is easiest when you have two painting partners working together: One applies the glaze, and the other does the dragging with a brush or comb. Use a poster board to experiment with the type of bristles and brushes you have on hand to create the desired effect.

As with any of the faux effects, subtle neutrals produce a refined, low-key look whereas bold hues create a casual, high-energy style. For dragging, you can use two related colors, such as pale yellow over gold, or two contrasting colors, such as pale blue over buff. For ideas, check out the many brochures available in home improvement or paint stores. Some paint manufacturers have already worked out fail-safe color combinations that you may want to consider.

1. Prep the room according to the instructions in Chapter 2, and apply a base coat of satin finish latex paint (see Chapter 4 for base coat how-to information). Let it dry at least 4 hours to overnight. Leave on any blue painter's tape, and tape any additional areas such as the ceiling, tops of door casings, or bottoms of window casings as needed.

2. Start in one corner of the room and use the 4-foot level to measure over 3 feet horizontally. Starting at the ceiling and going down toward the baseboard, make a perpendicular reference line from the 3-foot point and mark it approximately every 2 feet with blue painter's tape. Repeat this process all the way around the room, making sure that your lines are level.

3. Put on latex gloves. In a bucket, combine glaze with the other paint color (follow the manufacturer's instructions). Stir well with a stir stick, and pour the glaze mixture into a roller tray.

4. Starting in the most inconspicuous corner and up near the ceiling, cut in using your mini-roller; roll glaze along the ceiling line, down the corner, and across the top of the baseboard (cut in about 1¼ to 2 feet). Work in a 3- to 5-foot wide section. *Note:* It may be necessary to use a small chip brush to work glaze into tight corners.

5. Working quickly and with a zigzag motion, roll on the glaze using your mini-roller in the area you cut in. There's no need to be precise with the rolling; the important part is to keep the glaze wet so that you can create the best effect.

6. Starting at the top corner near the ceiling, place the tips of a clean 3-inch dragging brush (or comb) on the wall. (Use a pencil-grip, mentioned in Chapter 4, if you want maximum control over speed and pressure.) Drag the brush down the wall in one continuous stroke, keeping in line with your marked level lines.

For stronger lines, use more pressure; and for softer lines, use less pressure.

7. Clean off the brush at the end of the pass by wiping it on a clean rag.

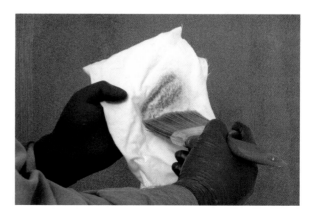

8. Repeat Steps 6 and 7, dragging over the area cut in and rolled in Steps 4 and 5. Switch to a clean rag when the one you're using can no longer remove the excess paint from your dragging brush.

9. When you come to the edge of the rolled section, place your cleaned-off brush at the ceiling line with a 1- to 2-inch overlap onto the wet edge of glaze. Drag the brush down the wall in one motion.

10. Repeat the application of glaze (cutting in and rolling on) and dragging off in 3- to 5-foot wide sections of wall.

TIP

For more complexity, place the brush at the ceiling line and drag downward to the halfway point. Clean off the brush with a dry rag. Then place the cleaned brush at the baseboard and drag upward to meet the downward lines at the halfway point. For visual variety, you can also stagger the points where the two directions meet.

TIP

For linen and denim effects, drag the brush through the glaze vertically. Let it dry for 20 minutes, and then apply a second coat of glaze. Drag the glaze off horizontally. Wipe the brush off on a clean rag after each pass.

Dragging on Wavy Lines

Stuff You Need to Know

Toolbox:

- Tools and materials for prep (see Chapter 2)
- Tools and materials for base coat (see Chapter 4)
- Satin finish latex paint for base coat
- Roller tray and liners
- Shower squeegee
- Ruler
- Pencil
- Utility knife
- Latex gloves
- Bucket
- Satin finish latex paint for glaze
- Glaze
- Stir sticks
- Mini-roller
- Small chip brush
- Clean rags

Time Needed:

About a weekend

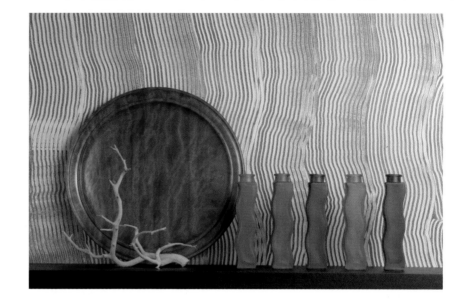

Dragging is a paint technique that involves applying a base coat and a glaze and then dragging over the glaze to subtract some of it and partially reveal the base coat. Dragging on wavy lines is the same as basic dragging (see the previous project in this chapter), but it creates a more whimsical look that may be appropriate for nurseries or children's rooms.

1. Prepare your room according to the instructions in Chapter 2. Apply a base coat of satin finish latex paint (see Chapter 4 for base coat how-to information). Let it dry at least 4 hours to overnight. Leave on any blue painter's tape, and tape any additional areas such as the ceiling, tops of door casings, or bottoms of window casings as needed.

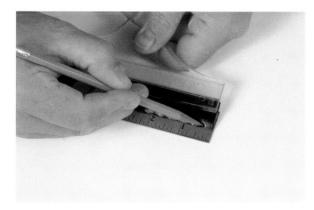

2. Lay the rubber blade of the shower squeegee against a ruler and use a pencil to mark off the placement of notches as desired for your design. You may want small notches for very fine lines, or you may want to mark wide, widely spaced notches for bolder lines.

3. With the squeegee blade flat on a cutting surface, use a utility knife to cut notches out of the blade where you marked it in Step 2.

4. Put on latex gloves. In the bucket, combine latex satin finish paint for glaze with the glaze (follow manufacturer's directions). Stir well with a stir stick, and pour the glaze mixture into a roller tray.

5. Starting in the most inconspicuous corner and up near the ceiling, cut in using your mini-roller; roll glaze along the ceiling line, down the corner, and across the top of the baseboard (cut in about 1¼ to 2 feet). Work in a 3- to 5-foot wide section. *Note:* It may be necessary to use a small chip brush to work glaze into tight corners.

6. Working quickly and with a zigzag motion, roll on the glaze using your mini-roller in the area you cut in. There's no need to be precise with the rolling; the important part is to keep the glaze wet so that you can create the best effect.

7. Drag the squeegee over the glaze in
the desired pattern, wiping it on a
clean rag after each pass on the wall.
For example, you may want wavy vertical lines, in which case you start at
the ceiling and drag the squeegee
down. Or you may want to drag the
squeegee across the glaze in a scal-
loped or swirled pattern.

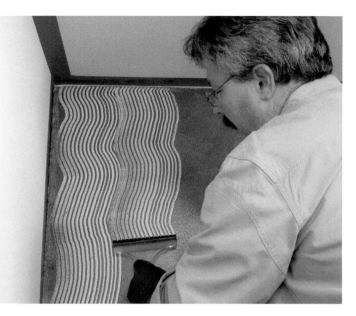

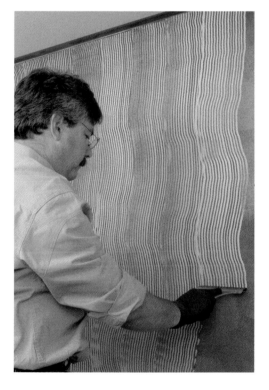

8. Repeat the application of glaze (cutting in
and rolling on) and dragging off with the
squeegee in 3- to 5-foot wide sections of wall.

Faux Leather Wall Finish

Stuff You Need to Know

Toolbox:

- Tools and materials for prep (see Chapter 2)
- Tools and materials for base coat (see Chapter 4)
- Eggshell finish latex paint for base coat
- Two roller covers
- Two roller cages
- Roller tray and liner
- 2-inch blue painter's tape
- 9-x-12-foot plastic drops, 1 mil thickness (enough to cover all walls being finished)
- Latex gloves
- Oil or latex glaze (tinted)
- 2-inch angled sash brush
- Mineral spirits
- Clean rags
- Krud Kutter

Time Needed:
About a weekend including overnight dry time

This classic finish creates a warm and interesting backdrop for any room, traditional or contemporary. For a traditional leather look, use a rich camel beige for your wall paint and a dark brown for the glaze layer. For a nontraditional look, try red and black, as shown here. You can actually use any color combination — just choose a lighter tone for the base color and a darker tone for the glaze. Make sure that the tones you choose coordinate with the fabrics and other furnishings in the room. Note that the glaze takes a long time to set up, but when it does, it's very durable. Still, you need to allow 24 hours for dry time at the end of this project.

1. Prep the room according to the instructions in Chapter 2. Cut in and roll on the eggshell finish base color (see Chapter 4 if you have any questions about painting a base coat). A second coat may be necessary if the walls have light spots or an uneven color tone. Let it dry completely, overnight if possible.

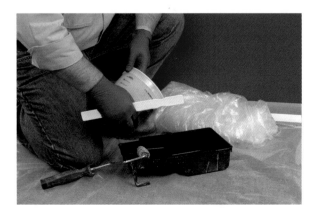

2. When you're ready for the glaze layer, unwrap one of the plastic drops and set it aside. Put on the latex gloves and pour about 2 cups of glaze into the roller tray.

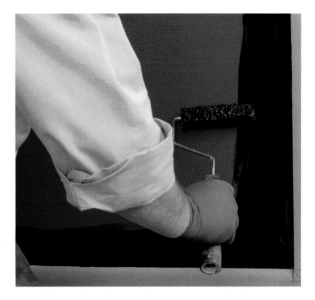

3. Doing only one wall at a time, paint on the glaze just like you did the paint. Cut in the edges with the 2-inch angled sash brush, and then use the roller for the rest. Make sure that you blend out any roller marks.

4. Pick up the 9-foot end of one of the plastic drops. Keep the bulk of the drop behind your body. Starting at an upper corner, press the plastic onto the wet wall with your hand. Don't pull it tight and flat; let it be a bit bunched up and wrinkled.

5. Continue along the ceiling until the top 1 to 2 feet of the plastic is loosely stuck to the wall. Be sure to keep the bulk of the drop away from the wall.

6. Loosely press the plastic onto the wall here and there all the way down to the floor. After the plastic touches the wall, don't pull it back off.

7. If your wall is wider than the plastic sheet, continue with another sheet of plastic cut to fit. If you have spaces that you didn't cover, don't try to re-position the plastic. Cut pieces of plastic that can be patched over those spots.

8. Using the clean roller, start at the top and roll out all the puffed out spaces in the plastic to press the plastic completely to the wall.

9. If any plastic is flopping around in the corners, cut it off or just tape the excess onto the plastic-covered wall to keep it out of your way.

10. Allow 2 to 4 hours for the plastic to slowly bond to the glaze. In the meantime, repeat the process on the next wall. Each wall should cure for the same amount of time.

11. When the plastic peels off with some resistance, it's ready to come off. Pull off the plastic and, as you pull, roll the plastic into a ball so that the glaze is inside. This technique contains the sticky side and the mess.

12. After you remove all the plastic, check for any missed spots. Fill in the spots with glaze. If you have a small spot, just dab on some glaze to take care of it. If you have a large spot, patch it with plastic and allow it to cure.

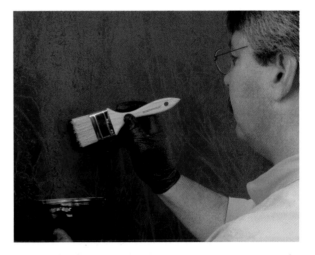

13. If you're using an oil glaze, wipe off any bleeds or drips before they dry by using some mineral spirits on a rag. If you're using a latex glaze, use a damp rag with a little bit of Krud Kutter on the rag.

When you're selecting glaze for this project, consider oil glaze, which allows for a longer window of work time, or latex glaze, which is more user-friendly when it comes to cleanup and odor. We tell you to use tinted glaze for convenience, but you can also tint the glaze yourself by mixing paint with glaze to get your desired color.

Ragging On

Stuff You Need to Know

Toolbox:
- ✔ Tools and materials for prep (see Chapter 2)
- ✔ Tools and materials for base coat (see Chapter 4)
- ✔ Eggshell or satin finish latex paint for base coat
- ✔ Latex gloves
- ✔ Two buckets
- ✔ Satin, eggshell, or semi-gloss finish latex paint for glaze
- ✔ Glaze
- ✔ Stir sticks
- ✔ Clean rags

Time Needed:
About a weekend, including overnight dry time

Rag rolling creates a textured look from only two colors. The two methods of ragging are positive (or ragging on), which we talk about here, and negative (or ragging off), which we discuss in the next project. For positive ragging, or ragging on, you apply glaze with a specialty roller or a rag to create your desired look. Basically, you soak a rag in glaze, wring it out, and then roll it over a base coat. Some people like to simply roll up the rag. Others like to wrap the rag around a roller and secure it with a string. Still others prefer to use a specially designed rag roller.

Try out your method, technique, and color combination on a test piece of poster board before committing to the real deal. If you're working alone, you have to work fast in order to achieve good results. As always, it's easier and faster to have your partner perform one function, such as rolling on the glaze, while you do another, such as ragging on.

To maximize your weekend project, do two opposing walls one day and the opposite walls the next day.

1. Prep the room according to the instructions in Chapter 2. Cut in and roll on a base coat (see Chapter 4) and let it dry overnight.

2. Put on latex gloves. In a bucket, pour satin finish latex paint (eggshell or semi-gloss will work as well) and add glaze. (Always follow the manufacturer's instructions for best results.) Stir these two together thoroughly with a stir stick until completely mixed.

3. Dip a rag into a bucket of clean water, and wring out the rag until it's slightly damp.

4. Load the rag by dipping it into your bucket full of glaze. Wring it out and arrange the rag like a crumpled ball in your hand.

5. Start in the least conspicuous area of the room, at the bottom of the wall, and roll upward. Roll the rag from your fingertips to the palm of your hand to the heel of your hand. Flip, rotate, and reshape the rag frequently to keep from creating a static pattern. Do a 3-by-3-foot area at a time.

6. While the glaze is still wet, stand back and examine the wall after completing one section. Does it seem too skimpy? Simply apply the rag where you need more color. Too much? Use a damp, clean rag to blot off the excess. Trying to fix a wall after the glaze dries can cause problems.

7. Rag and repeat. Start new sections and work from the dry onto the wet edge.

Ragging on can be very messy, so you should do the protective prep work covered in Chapter 2 as well as keep lots of rags on hand for cleanup.

Ragging Off

Negative ragging, or ragging off, includes painting a base coat on, letting it dry overnight, applying glaze with a roller, and removing the glaze with a rag, plastic baggy, cheesecloth, terry cloth towel, or some other similar material in order to create the desired look. Many people find that achieving their desired look is easier with ragging off than with ragging on (see the previous project). For best results, have a partner roll on the glaze while you pounce it off with a rag. If you don't have a partner to work with, make sure you roll just a small section so that the glaze doesn't dry before you have a chance to pounce it off.

1. Prep the room according to the instructions in Chapter 2. Cut in and roll on a base coat (see Chapter 4) and let it dry overnight.

2. Put on gloves, and combine the other paint and the glaze in a bucket and stir with a stir stick. (Always follow the manufacturer's instructions for their products for best results.) Pour some glaze into a roller tray.

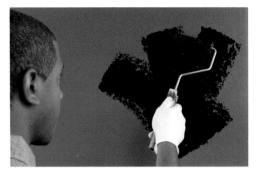

3. Use a mini-roller to roll glaze on the wall from the corner and ceiling to the base, working in sections about 3 feet wide. Work from the ceiling to the floor. Leave the edges random and jagged — you don't want a clean line.

4. Take your rag (plastic baggy, cheesecloth, terry cloth towel, or whatever material will give you your desired effect) and crumple it into a ball. Pounce the crumpled rag on top of the rolled-on glaze to remove some of the glaze. Turn the rag often to achieve a modeled look.

5. Repeat rolling the glaze on an adjacent 3-foot section of the wall. When you move to the next section, make sure to roll from the dry area ahead of you back toward the wet area you just completed, stopping about an inch short of the wet area.

6. Use a new, dry rag to pounce the current wet area, moving back to the previously completed area. Continue working toward the upper and lower unfinished corner of the wall until you've gone around the room.

7. Assess your work as you apply and rag off the glaze. Trying to manipulate the look after it dries can cause problems. If the area doesn't have enough glaze, let it become almost dry before you add more glaze and pounce it off again.

Sponging On

Sponging on creates surface interest. In this positive or additive technique, the base coat color dominates. Establishing a rhythm and working quickly is critical to creating a pleasing surface. Be sure to step back and examine each section from a distance. Correcting the effect when paint is wet is much easier than trying to make corrections after it dries.

For this and other sponge projects, work quickly and use even pressure. Keep the sponge moist with consistent amounts of paint, and use small sponges at the corners.

1. Prep the room according to the instructions in Chapter 2, and then cut in and roll on your base coat color (see Chapter 4 for instructions on applying a solid coat of paint). Let dry 4 to 6 hours or overnight.

2. In a bucket, combine the other paint with glaze according to the manufacturer's instructions. Mix it thoroughly with a stir stick.

3. Put on your latex gloves, wet the sea sponge, and wring out the excess water with a gentle twisting motion.

4. Dip the sponge into the glaze combination and then blot it on a paper towel. You're going to pounce the sponge onto the wall, and you want to avoid having a heavy beginning pounce and a light ending pounce. The key is to keep a consistent amount of glaze on the sponge at all times so that the overall look of the wall is consistent.

5. Starting at the top of the wall and working toward the bottom, lightly touch the wall with the sponge and then twist your hand as you pull the sponge away from the wall. Don't hit the wall — if you do, the paint from the sponge will create a blob on the spot you hit.

6. Complete one 3-foot section of the wall by turning the sponge frequently and spacing the pounces well apart with the sponge twisted at different angles — you want to create an abstract pattern on the wall.

7. Move on to the next 3-foot section of the wall, and then continue around the room. Make sure you slightly overlap your sections so that you don't end up with a blank area between sections.

Create greater dimensionality by applying a second glaze color. Wait about 20 minutes after completing your first glaze color to sponge on the second color — just use the same steps. Overlap the colors randomly. For even more drama, sponge on a third glaze color, repeating the steps and overlapping the sponging.

Sponging Off

Stuff You Need to Know

Toolbox:

- Tools and materials for prep (see Chapter 2)
- Tools and materials for base coat (see Chapter 4)
- Satin, matte, or eggshell finish latex paint for base coat
- Two buckets
- Satin or eggshell finish latex paint for glaze
- Glaze
- Stir sticks
- Three or more sea sponges
- Sharp scissors or knife
- Latex gloves
- Roller cover
- Roller cage
- Paint tray

Time Needed:

About a weekend plus overnight dry time

In this subtractive technique, the glaze color dominates over the base color. Drama comes from combining warm and cool colors or light and dark colors. Subtlety comes from using closely related colors (orange and yellow, or green and blue) and from compatible neutrals (white and beige). As with any glaze, you must work quickly while the glaze is still wet. To ensure wetness, work in small sections and work closely with your partner, if you have one.

1. Prep the room according to the instructions in Chapter 2, and then cut in and roll on your base coat (see Chapter 4 for details on applying a base coat). Let it dry overnight. If you want to use a pre-existing base coat, you can skip this step.

2. In a bucket, combine the other paint and glaze according to the manufacturer's instructions. Stir thoroughly with a stir stick and pour the combination into a paint tray.

3. Prepare your sea sponges by cutting them in half lengthwise with sharp scissors or a knife. Cut one of the halves in half and use the small sponges for cutting in at corners, ceiling, baseboards, and so on.

4. Put on latex gloves, dampen the sponge that you're getting ready to use, and squeeze it out into a bucket of water.

5. Start in the least noticeable corner of the room and roll on the glaze in a section no wider than two roller widths. Go from floor to ceiling, using the "M" technique (see Chapter 4 for this technique).

6. Hold your sponge in your dominant hand, press the sponge on the wall, and quickly pull it off the surface in a pouncing motion to sponge off the glaze. Repeat the pouncing motion, changing your wrist position and angle of your arm to remove the glaze in a random pattern. Turn the sponge over after every five pounces. Rinse and wring out your sponge every couple of minutes.

7. Roll the next section of glaze by working from the dry area and overlapping the wet edge ever so slightly. Repeat the pouncing off motion from the previous step. Step back and analyze your work as you go. Use clean, damp sponges to rework over sections to create pleasing effects that are random in pattern but consistent with respect to the amount of glaze being subtracted. Continue around the room.

Combine sponging off and sponging on techniques. After you sponge off your glaze, you can sponge on some sheer glaze in a metallic or light shade to create gleaming highlights.

Chambray

Give your walls the casual, cozy feel of your favorite summer pants with a simple technique that makes walls mimic lightweight chambray fabric. The soft pattern provides depth but doesn't demand all the attention in the room and works well as an allover pattern for an entire room.

1. Prepare the room according to the instructions in Chapter 2. Cut in and roll on your lighter base coat (see Chapter 4 for details). Apply a second coat if you need one. Let the paint dry completely, preferably overnight.

2. Choose the wall(s) you want to glaze, and then measure sections 3 feet wide across those wall(s). Use the level and yardstick to create straight vertical lines.

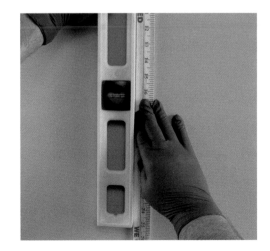

3. Mark off vertical lines for each section by running the colored pencil along the yardstick.

4. Tape off every other section by pressing the painter's tape firmly along the lines you drew in Step 3.

5. Put on latex gloves, and mix together the acrylic glaze and the darker color paint in a bucket according to package instructions. Stir with a stir stick. Make sure you mix a batch that's more than big enough to complete your project. Matching the exact consistency is extremely hard.

6. Keep the gloves on, pour some of the glaze mixture into a roller tray, and use a roller to apply glaze to one 3-foot section of wall.

7. Move the 12-inch wallpaper brush lightly across the glazed section in horizontal strokes, working from top to bottom. Work swiftly so that the glaze stays wet, and wipe off the brush tips regularly on a damp rag.

8. After you reach the bottom of the glazed section, wipe the brush again and work top to bottom, making light vertical strokes with the brush.

9. Immediately remove the tape from the finished section.

10. Repeat Steps 6 through 9 on the rest of the taped sections. When you complete this step, every other section of your wall will have the chambray effect.

11. Seal your remaining paint-glaze mixture in an airtight container. Allow the glazed wall to dry overnight.

12. Tape the unfinished sections and repeat Steps 6 through 9 until each section has been glazed and brushed.

Bagging

Ordinary plastic grocery bags step up to the challenge of creating interesting wall effects. The crumpled bags add depth with sharp "veins" etched into the paint. Bagging is a great project for beginners and for budget-minded decorators because the primary tool is one you probably already have on hand.

1. Prep the room according to the instructions in Chapter 2. Put on a base coat of paint and let it dry completely. Add a second coat if necessary for coverage. Check out Chapter 4 for directions for basic wall painting.

2. Wearing gloves, combine in a bucket the acrylic glaze and your contrasting-color paint according to the manufacturer's instructions. Stir the glaze thoroughly using a stir stick, and pour it into the paint tray.

   Make sure you mix a batch more than big enough to complete your project because mixing a new batch with the exact consistency of the previous one is no easy feat.

3. Starting in the most inconspicuous corner and up near the ceiling, cut in using your mini-roller; roll glaze along the ceiling line, down the corner, and across the top of the baseboard (cut in about 1¼ to 2 feet). Work in a 3-foot wide section. (*Note:* It may be necessary to use a small chip brush to work glaze into tight corners.)

4. Working quickly and with a zigzag motion, roll on the glaze using your mini-roller in the area you cut in. There's no need to be precise with the rolling; the important part is to keep the glaze wet so that you can create the best effect.

5. Turn a bag inside out (so that none of the ink on the outside transfers onto your walls), and loosely crumple it up.

6. Dab the crumpled bag lightly onto the glazed surface. Simply press it into the wet glaze and then pull it back without smearing the glaze.

7. Continue pressing the bag into the glaze, turning it regularly to keep the pattern random and overlapping into previously bagged spots. Grab a new bag when the old one becomes too coated with glaze to leave an impression.

8. Repeat Steps 3 through 7 until the entire room has been bagged.

Use thicker bags if you want deeper veins in the paint; heavier plastic or even paper grocery bags help you achieve that effect. Use plastic wrap instead of bags if you want delicate veins.

Frottage

Stuff You Need to Know

Toolbox:

- ✔ Tools and materials for prep (see Chapter 2)
- ✔ Tools and materials for base coat (see Chapter 4)
- ✔ Eggshell finish latex paint in two shades of the same color
- ✔ Brown paper (mailing paper, grocery bags, or unprinted newspaper)
- ✔ Latex gloves
- ✔ Acrylic glaze
- ✔ Bucket
- ✔ Stir sticks
- ✔ Roller tray and liners
- ✔ Roller cover
- ✔ Roller cage

Time Needed:
About a weekend

Use glaze that's just a shade off your base color for a subtle crackled effect, or get bold with two colors that are several shades apart. The delicate veins that frottage creates can complement either approach.

1. Prep the room according to instructions in Chapter 2, and paint on the darker color of paint as the base (see Chapter 4 for more on painting a base coat). Let the base coat dry at least 4 hours to overnight. Apply a second coat if necessary for good coverage, and let dry. Leave up any tape or masking.

2. Tear the brown paper into roughly 3-by-3-foot squares (or open the grocery bags so that they're flat and only one sheet thick).

3. Crumple each piece of brown paper, and then flatten it out but don't smooth out the wrinkles.

4. Wearing latex gloves, combine the lighter top color and glaze in a bucket according to the manufacturer's instructions, and stir before pouring some of the mixture into a roller tray.

5. Working in approximately 3-foot sections, paint on the glaze using a roller. *Note:* Glaze a slightly bigger section than you can cover with a sheet of paper so that you can overlap the edges without reglazing.

6. Working quickly so that the glaze doesn't have a chance to dry, press a crumpled sheet of brown paper onto the glazed area of wall. The sheet generally should be square with the wall, not askew. Gently smooth the sheet into the wall with your palm.

7. Gently pull the sheet of paper straight away from the wall. It should take some of the glaze with it, leaving a veiny effect.

8. Repeat Steps 5 through 7 until you've worked across the entire wall or room, overlapping the paper with the previous frottaged section as you go.

TIP

One person can handle this project by working in sections, but you can work a lot faster with another pair of hands on the job. When you work with a partner, one person rolls on the glaze and the other follows with the paper.

Chapter 7
More Fun Decorative Techniques

Tasks performed in this chapter
- ✔ Texturing on suede
- ✔ Venetian plaster
- ✔ Painted tissue wallpaper
- ✔ Gradient
- ✔ Stippling

Try the fun, decorative techniques in this chapter when you want those unique elements that make your home the envy of the neighborhood. Catch the eye of any guest by transforming often-ignored, low-traffic areas into the height of elegance and sophistication. For concrete ideas on where and when to use the five techniques we show you in this chapter, check out the following list:

✔ For elegance, nothing compares to a suede finish. It works beautifully in a guest room, large foyer, library, office, or den. The slightly rough surface makes washing off finger marks difficult, so try it in adults-only areas.

✔ You can use Venetian plaster to create several looks and textures. This centuries-old technique can give walls a classic, polished look; or you can achieve a contemporary appearance by adding metallic tones to the plaster compound. Use it when you want to hide surface imperfections on wood, drywall, stone, brick, and other surfaces.

✔ Painted tissue wallpaper gives your space or surface three-dimensions and an entirely new look. You end up with a crinkled look that effectively covers up any imperfections. This finish is ideal for low-traffic areas.

✔ A gradient finish in a small room or below a chair rail can make you feel as though you're living with a sunset. If you want to try the technique in a large room, put the gradient finish on just one wall to add visual interest.

✔ Stippling is best in small areas because it takes a long time to achieve the effect. Consider using it on an accent wall, in a breakfast nook, or on something as small as a door or window frame.

TIP

If you're interested in trying a faux finish technique, but you're not ready to commit to an entire wall, try the technique on a picture frame or table first. Or try a large piece of poster board for practice. When you get the feel for the process and confirm that you like the results, you'll be more confident applying the technique to your furniture or walls. After you do one faux finish project, you'll be much more confident about trying any of the others.

Texturing on Suede

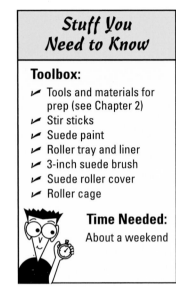

Created with specialty rollers and paints, this faux technique mimics the soft, supple look of suede. Its slightly rough surface doesn't stand up to wear and tear or washing, so use this technique only in low-traffic spaces such as a home office or guest room.

You can use the same color paint for the base coat and finish coat (as this project does), or you can opt for multiple base and finish colors for more drama. A third option is using lighter and darker values of the same color to add dimension.

1. Prepare the room and walls according to instructions in Chapter 2.

2. Stir the suede paint thoroughly and pour it into the roller tray.

3. Use the 3-inch suede brush to cut in around windows, doors, switches and outlets, and the perimeter of the room. Cut in approximately the width of the brush.

4. Roll paint on all walls vertically (not in an "M" pattern) with a special suede roller. The coat will look uneven, but you shouldn't touch it up. Overworking the drying paint will ruin the finish and be very noticeable. Allow this first coat of paint to dry completely, at least 4 hours.

5. Use a 3-inch suede brush to crosshatch on the second coat of paint. Use overlapping, random length strokes, and reposition your wrist and arm frequently to vary your stroke and angles. Work fast, starting at the top of the wall and sweeping your strokes down the wall. Also work from dry to wet areas, but don't overlap wet paint onto drying paint.

Venetian Plaster

Use Venetian plaster to create a random texture that has an air of classical architecture about it. The effect dresses plain old plywood or plaster walls in a cloak of natural stone — or so it would appear. You make it happen by smearing Venetian plaster willy-nilly over the surface. Doing so hides small blemishes in the walls.

You can buy Venetian plaster in pre-tinted gallon buckets or in versions that require you (or a staffer at the store where you buy it) to add tint. You get a lot more room to play around with color if you choose the latter.

1. Prep the room according to the instructions in Chapter 2.

2. Use the 40- to 60-grit sandpaper to file down the edges of your steel trowel. Doing so helps prevent scratches and gouges in the plaster.

3. Put on latex gloves, and use the steel trowel to apply plaster in a thin coat. Start in a corner, and use long and short strokes that crisscross over each other at varying angles. Don't worry about covering the entire wall; leaving small bare spots as you apply the first coat is preferable.

4. Wipe the trowel clean with a damp rag after every other application of plaster.

5. Continue applying plaster until you move across the entire wall.
   Remember: You're not covering every bit of wall at this point. Small bits of wall show through the first coat of plaster.

6. Let the plaster dry completely. Four to five hours should do the trick, but consult the plaster instructions.

7. Wearing gloves, apply a second thin coat of plaster by using the steel trowel and the same crisscross technique. Make sure you cover the entire wall, leaving no gaps or low spots.

8. Apply a third coat in the same fashion if you want to. Doing so makes the plaster stronger and the texture deeper, but you can stop with two coats and get a great-looking wall.

9. Let the final coat dry overnight.

10. Use 600-grit sandpaper to polish the plaster by rubbing it in large circles. Start in an upper corner and work across the entire wall.

11. Wipe down the wall with a damp rag to remove grit.

Because Venetian plaster can be used to create a wide range of textures, make sure you play around with it a bit before getting started on the wall you plan to texture. Different thicknesses, strategies for applying the plaster, and number of coats you use give very different results. Changing stream halfway through the project yields a mishmash of a wall. Venetian plaster looks best when you achieve an even texture throughout the area you cover.

Painted Tissue Wallpaper

Stuff You Need to Know

Toolbox:

- ✔ Tools and materials for prep (see Chapter 2)
- ✔ Plain white tissue paper (unused)
- ✔ Latex gloves
- ✔ Ready-to-use wallpaper adhesive
- ✔ Roller tray and liners
- ✔ Two roller covers
- ✔ Roller cage
- ✔ Soft-bristled paintbrush, any size
- ✔ Semi-gloss finish latex paint
- ✔ Stir sticks
- ✔ 2-inch angled sash brush

Time Needed:
About a weekend

Plain old tissue paper is a gift to walls, giving them a hypnotic crinkle effect. The look is easy to create and great for covering imperfections in walls. Stop with just a layer of paint or, if you want to bring more attention to the texture of the walls, finish with a glaze two shades darker than your paint. (Turn to Chapter 6 for more about glazing.)

This project is a great choice if you don't want to take the time to apply a base coat of paint. The painted tissue paper covers the surface completely, so it doesn't matter what color the wall is underneath!

1. Prepare the room and walls according to the instructions in Chapter 2.

2. Crumple each sheet of tissue paper, and then spread out and stack the sheets without smoothing out all the wrinkles.

3. Put on latex gloves, and pour some wallpaper adhesive into a roller tray.

4. Starting in an upper corner in the least conspicuous area of the room, roll wallpaper adhesive on the wall from floor to ceiling in an area about 3 feet wide.

5. Press one sheet of tissue paper onto an area of wet wallpaper adhesive, and smooth it gently with your hand or a soft brush. Take care not to smooth out all the wrinkles though!

6. Place the next sheet of tissue paper onto the wet adhesive so that it overlaps the previous sheet slightly.

7. Repeat Steps 4 through 6 until the walls are covered with tissue paper. Let it dry overnight.

8. Paint the tissue papered walls in your desired paint color. Use a 2-inch angled sash brush to cut in gently along the ceiling and baseboards and around doors and windows so as not to damage the paper. Then roll on paint. (Refer to Chapter 4 for basic painting instructions.)

Buy at least 25 percent more tissue paper than you need to cover the square footage you plan to paint. You need some extra for overlap and for "better safe than sorry" purposes.

Painting a Gradient

Mimic the effect of the sun by giving walls a gradient. With this technique, you start with dark paint low on the wall and lighten the paint as you progress up the wall. The result is an intriguing look that has a warm, worn-in feeling — like an old pair of blue jeans.

Because you work this effect in sections and use multiple coats of three different colors, it's a good one for smaller walls or in the space between a chair rail and the floor.

1. Prepare the room according to the instructions in Chapter 2, and apply the light shade of paint as the base (see Chapter 4 for base coat instructions).

2. Wearing latex gloves, in each bucket mix each of the remaining three paint colors with glaze in a ratio of two parts glaze to one part paint. Stir with stir sticks. You want a fairly transparent mixture.

3. With a 4-inch flat brush, paint on the darkest color of glaze from the bottom of the wall to the halfway point. Don't end with a straight line across the wall. Instead, brush past the halfway point in some spots and not quite up to it in others. An uneven line works much better for this effect than a precise one.

4. Using a clean 4-inch flat brush, begin applying the medium shade of glaze so that it blends into the dark shade on the bottom and extends up past it about a foot. Again, work so that you create a jagged line. In some spots you may pull the paint up only 6 inches and in others it may extend 18 inches above the darker color.

5. Using a clean 4-inch flat brush, apply the light shade of glaze, starting at the top of the wall or area and working down into the medium shade. Blend the colors a bit by painting into the medium paint with the light color. Work so that you create a jagged edge between the two colors.

6. Let the paint dry for 4 to 6 hours.

7. Wash your brushes as described in Chapter 4.

8. Using a clean 4-inch flat brush, paint the medium shade of glaze along the middle strip of color. Follow the same process as in Step 4, working quickly so that the paint doesn't have time to dry and you can adequately blend it.

9. Using a clean 4-inch flat brush, paint the dark shade of glaze along the bottom strip of color. Follow the same process as in Step 3, working quickly and blending the color.

10. Using a clean 4-inch flat brush, paint the light shade of glaze along the top strip of color. Follow the same process as in Step 5, working quickly to blend the paint.

11. Let paint dry. If necessary, repeat Steps 8 through 10 until you achieve a smooth, subtle transition from one shade to the next.

Stippling

Stuff You Need to Know

Toolbox:

- Tools and materials for prep (see Chapter 2)
- Tools and materials or base coat (see Chapter 4)
- Latex gloves
- Stir sticks
- Latex paint in light, medium, and dark shades of the same color
- Three small paint containers
- Stippling brush
- Colorwashing brush

Time Needed:

About a day

To achieve a *stippled* effect, you apply small points, dots, or dabs of paint to your surface. Given that a stippling brush covers just a few square inches and your walls are many, many square feet, stippling is a project for the patient painter.

1. Prepare the room and walls according to the instructions in Chapter 2, and apply a base coat of the lightest shade of paint (see Chapter 4 for base coat instructions). Let it dry at least 4 hours to overnight.

2. Put on gloves, and use stir sticks to stir all three shades of paint. Pour some of each into three small containers.

3. Begin stippling with the medium-colored paint. Use the colorwashing brush to stipple corners, and use the stipple brush to stipple the flat areas of the wall. With either brush, the technique is the same: Dip the tip of the brush into the medium tone paint, and then apply it to the wall by popping your wrist so that the bristles hit the wall straight on and then bounce back, depositing tiny dots of paint. Change the angle of the brush as you move across a section in long, wavy lines. (The size of the section is determined when you run out of paint.)

4. When the brush runs out of paint, clean the bristles on a clean, dry rag.

5. Repeat Step 3 with the light shade of paint, stippling so that the light tone overlaps in places with the medium one. (The colors mix at the point of overlap, creating a lot of depth on the wall.)

6. When the brush runs out of paint, clean it on a rag, and repeat Step 3 with the dark shade of paint.

7. Repeat Steps 3 through 6 until you finish the entire wall or room.

For stippling with a subtle effect, use just two very close shades of the same color paint: one as a base color and the other stippled over it.

Part III
Covering Other Areas of Your Home

The 5th Wave By Rich Tennant

"The only thing I can figure is you used floor paint on the ceiling."

In this part . . .

*I*t takes more than just four walls to create a room. But you probably think of those walls first when you decide to add a fresh coat of paint to spruce up your living space. In this part, we urge you not to neglect the other areas of your home. Unfortunately, ceilings with peeling paint and well-worn floors can detract from your beautifully painted walls. Fortunately, painting ceilings and floors is just another project for the courageous do-it-yourselfer.

Same goes for your trim (including baseboards and molding) and your windows and doors. A fresh coat of paint can do wonders, and we tell you what you need to know to tackle these all-too-often neglected areas.

Chapter 8

Coating Ceilings and Floors

Tasks performed in this chapter

- ✔ Painting a smooth ceiling
- ✔ Painting coffered ceilings
- ✔ Painting wood floors
- ✔ Painting concrete floors

When you want to paint your walls, take a good look at the ceiling too. Can you really get away with not painting it? No, not if it looks gray and dingy, or if it's water stained or yellowed by age or nicotine. Painting overhead is literally a pain in the neck, even when you use a roller with an extension handle. Opting for the alternative, however, detracts from the elegance of your freshly painted walls; the new wall paint can actually make the ceiling look worse than it is. So consider adding ceiling paint to your shopping list.

Sometimes when you plan to paint the walls, however, the ceiling's in good shape. Paint it anyway if you want to give a dead white ceiling a little color, if the color that's on the ceiling makes the room appear smaller than it is, or if you're tempted to duck every time you go into the room (that happens when the ceiling height is 8 feet or less and the color is darker than the color of the walls).

Homeowners paint concrete floors to give them a finished look at a relatively low cost and to reduce the amount of dust that comes off unfinished concrete. You can paint wood floors too. In fact, you can paint just about any type of flooring that's beginning to look tired or worn for far less money than it costs to purchase another floor covering. You can be creative with paint by stenciling or painting traditional or whimsical borders on the floor, or by using several colors to paint designs or even a game board. When you tire of the floor, just roll on another coat of primer and paint it all over again. In the meantime, read up on painting floors in the following pages.

Prepping Ceilings and Floors

Ceilings and floors are no different than walls: Before you paint, you have to prep. This section helps you determine what kind of prep work you need to do. Most of the techniques will probably seem familiar. If the introduction to this chapter convinced you to paint your ceiling, read through this checklist and decide what needs to be done:

- ✔ If you have a plaster ceiling, repair cracks before you start priming and painting.
- ✔ If you see grease on the ceiling, wash the surface thoroughly.

✔ If a drywall ceiling has been soaked by water, cut out the affected area and replace it with new drywall.

✔ If the ceiling has water or nicotine discoloration or stains, prime it before painting.

✔ If the existing ceiling paint has a lot of sheen and you want to cover it with latex paint, prime it first. Primer leaves a rough surface the paint can stick to.

✔ If the existing ceiling looks good, but you want to change the color or add another coat of paint, prime it first. When paint adheres to the surface, it goes on smoother and looks more even. So using a primer makes good sense even if the ceiling doesn't have any of the obvious problems in this list.

Painting the floor gives you an opportunity to show off your flair and creativity without spending a lot of money. But you want your canvas to be in the best possible shape before you get started; otherwise, your new design will look less than stellar. Wood and concrete are the most commonly painted floors, and each surface requires a little different prep work.

To prep wood floors, follow these instructions:

1. **Clean.** Clean the floor thoroughly. Get rid of grease, grime, wax, and anything else that has built up on the surface.

2. **Fill.** If the wood is splintered or gouged, fill in those areas with a tinted wood filler.

3. **Sand.** If the wood is rough, sand it smooth with 120-grit sandpaper. If previously finished wood is glossy, sand it with 120-grit sandpaper.

4. **Scrape.** Scrape off cracked or loose paint on previously finished wood floors, and then feather the finished and scraped areas to make a smooth surface.

5. **Prime.** Use a latex or alkyd primer under latex paint. Use an oil-based primer under oil-based or polyurethane paint. Unfinished wood floors soak up a lot of paint, so priming is important.

6. **Select your paint.** If you want a satin finish on the wood, use a quality latex paint. If you want a semi-gloss or gloss finish, use latex, alkyd, or polyurethane paint.

To prep concrete floors, follow these instructions:

1. **Patch.** If the concrete floor has any surface cracks or imperfections, use a concrete filler, and then sand the patches smooth.

2. **Clean.** Scrub the floor thoroughly with TSP to remove grease, dirt, and anything else (such as carpet tape) that has built up on the surface.

3. **Wash and dry.** Rinse the floor several times and let it dry thoroughly. A concrete floor can take up to three days to dry.

4. **Sand.** Sand off imperfections using 80-grit sandpaper.

5. **Sweep it up.** Vacuum the floor thoroughly.

6. **Prime.** You want to prime any floor that has an uneven texture or is porous. Bare concrete is extremely porous, so priming is extremely important.

Do-it-yourself do's for cleaning ceilings

As you prepare a ceiling for painting, be sure to follow these tips:

✔ Do use a non-skid, moisture-proof drop-cloth to cover the floor, and make sure that you securely tape it in place. If it's non-skid, you can concentrate on hand-work, not footwork, and a moisture-proof barrier prevents liquids from seeping through to the floor.

✔ Do wear goggles and protective cloth-ing, including a head covering, to protect your skin from strong detergents and paint products. Tape the cuffs of a long-sleeved shirt so that nothing runs under the sleeves.

✔ Do use a short-handled squeegee to remove excess water so that the surface dries quickly.

✔ Don't overload your sponge, if you're using one. Drips increase cleanup time and cause paint to spread unevenly.

✔ Do divide the ceiling into strips or areas and progress from one to the next in an orderly fashion in order to thoroughly cover the ceiling. (Note: You don't have to tape off the areas — just eyeball them.)

✔ Do use a sturdy stepladder, preferably one with wide treads to keep you from slipping off the rungs.

Popcorn ceiling considerations

Popcorn ceilings are textured, acoustic ceilings that are sprayed on and resemble popcorn or cottage cheese when they dry. Home builders typically put in popcorn ceilings because it's an inexpensive and fast way to finish a room. The additive that gives the paint its texture is fragile; it melts when it gets wet, and it can wipe off onto the roller. Even sweeping a popcorn ceiling can loosen the additive. So if you paint a popcorn ceiling, be sure to use the fewest paint strokes possible and paint in only one direction to minimize the amount of stuff raining down on your head. Alternately, you can spray on the paint.

If you're thinking about removing the popcorn, keep these things in mind:

✔ If an acoustic spray was used in a home built before 1980, the popcorn ceilings contain asbestos. Before you begin, check to see whether the ceiling contains asbestos. If it does, cover it with a new coat of acoustic spray instead of remov-ing it, which potentially can make the asbestos airborne.

Warning: Removing asbestos, a haz-ardous material when tiny particles become airborne and are inhaled, is a costly procedure that local governments generally tightly control. Licensed tech-nicians wearing "space suits and masks" have to remove the asbestos from public buildings and can take it only to approved disposal sites. Generally you can encap-sulate or surround the asbestos without disturbing it and without it becoming a health hazard. But to be safe, wear your breathing mask, goggles, a long-sleeved shirt, and long pants, and cover your hair.

✔ Painting over popcorn makes the water-soluble stuff hard to remove later on. So, if you're going to remove the popcorn, do it before you paint your room.

✔ Removing popcorn isn't an easy job; you have to scrape, sand, apply Skim Coat (a smooth-finish base coat), and then apply the finish paint. Sometimes removing the popcorn isn't practical because of the time, effort, and cost.

Painting a Smooth Ceiling

If you're painting a whole room, paint the ceiling before you paint the walls or trim. To get the best results on ceilings, prep by cleaning off dust with a broom and fixing any problems like stains and mildew (see Chapter 2 for cleaning how-to's) and cracked plaster or popped nails on drywall (turn to Chapter 3 for more on these repairs).

As for paint, use ceiling paint, which is formulated to spatter less, diffuse light more evenly, and have an even, flat sheen. If desired, you can have the paint technician tint the ceiling paint to coordinate with your wall paint (most painters use a 25 percent tint).

Paint the town red and the ceiling pink

Getting even coverage on ceilings can be tough because you're working overhead and it's hard to see variations or skipped spots on previously painted ceilings. A product that eliminates this problem is pink ceiling paint that dries white. The pink tint when it's wet makes it easier to spot missed spots and imperfections when you're rolling it on. You can get more information from a paint specialist at your local home improvement or paint store. **Note:** It's possible to tint regular ceiling paint, but this variety that rolls on pink is only available in a white finished color.

1. Prep the room according to the instructions in Chapter 2, placing dropcloths on the floor and taping the walls where they meet the ceiling with 2-inch blue painter's tape.

2. Stir the ceiling paint thoroughly and pour some into the tray.

3. Starting in the corner farthest from the door on the narrowest wall, cut in the edges of the ceiling with a 2-inch sash brush. Cut in only small sections of wall at a time, about 3 to 6 feet.

4. Wearing a hat and goggles and using a roller attached to an extension handle, paint a roughly 3-foot diagonal line on the ceiling to unload paint from the roller.

5. Distribute paint by rolling the roller over the diagonal line back and forth, not side to side, in the direction of the diagonal line. Start each new stroke by slightly overlapping the previous stroke.

6. On the final stroke before reloading the roller, roll toward the door.

7. Repeat Steps 3 through 6 all the way around the ceiling.

Have plain white acoustic ceilings? Paint those tiles with tinted ceiling paint to make them more attractive. What you lose in sound reduction you make up for in looks! Lots of restaurants paint their acoustic ceilings black or dark brown to make them seem to disappear, but you may want to opt for a color that coordinates with your wall color for a cozy effect.

Pretreat stained areas on the ceiling by priming them with an oil-based sealer. Check out Chapter 4 for information on priming and sealing.

Painting Wood Floors

Stuff You Need to Know

Toolbox:

- ✔ Vacuum cleaner
- ✔ Latex gloves
- ✔ TSP or TSP-PF
- ✔ Bucket
- ✔ Sponge mop
- ✔ 2-inch blue painter's tape
- ✔ Stir sticks
- ✔ Primer or combination primer/sealer if the floor has knots or stains
- ✔ 2½-inch synthetic angled sash brush
- ✔ Telescoping extension pole
- ✔ Two roller covers
- ✔ Roller cage
- ✔ Roller tray and liners
- ✔ Paint

Time Needed:

About a day

Laminate long gone? Poor quality wood flooring? Then painting is your best — and cheapest — option for making your wood floor look its best. You can use interior paint (or enamel for a harder finish) or specially formulated floor paint. Floor paints come both ready- and custom-mixed and in gloss or satin finishes, too.

Keep in mind that latex paint, although easy to apply and widely available, doesn't stand up to heavy wear and tear. Alkyd paints perform better on floors because they dry to a hard finish, cover well, and stand up to moderate foot traffic. Epoxy paints and industrial enamels cover extremely well and stand up to heavy foot traffic but are available in fewer colors.

1. Remove furniture and rugs, and vacuum the floor.

2. Put on latex gloves, and follow the manufacturer's instruction to combine TSP or
   TSP-PF solution with water in a bucket. Use
   a sponge mop to clean the floor with the
   solution. (For greasy floors, apply degreaser
   with clean cloth or sponge mop; follow the
   manufacturer's instructions for use.)

3. Use painter's tape to tape bottom
   edge of baseboards or wall to protect them from paint spatters and
   unintended brush or roller marks.

4. Stir primer with a stir stick. Starting in the
   corner farthest from the door, cut in the corners of the floor with a 2½-inch sash brush.

5. Roll on primer or a combination sealer/primer using a long-handled extension pole to speed up the job and save your back. Work in 4-foot-square areas. Let the floor dry thoroughly according to the primer manufacturer's instructions. (It can take from 30 minutes to a couple hours.)

6. Use a stir stick to stir the finish paint thoroughly, and pour some of it into a roller tray (about 2 inches of paint in the well of the tray).

7. Use a 2½-inch sash brush to cut in the finish paint around the perimeter of the room.

8. Starting in the corner farthest from the door, roll on the finish paint using a roller at the end of an extension pole.

9. Let the paint dry overnight before walking on it. It's best to let it cure for several days before moving in furniture or rugs.

If you can see any imperfections on the floor after cleaning it, use 180-grit sandpaper to remove them. The smoother the floor, the nicer your project will look when it's finished.

You can paint almost any floor surface — linoleum, vinyl, or tile. If you're looking for a short-term solution, painting is the way to go. Just be sure to prep the surface (by cleaning, sanding, and even deglossing) and prime it as you would any hard-to-paint surface.

Painting Concrete Floors

Concrete requires extra prep for painting because of its coarse texture and porosity. Masonry paints are designed for concrete, and some are intended specifically for use on floors and stairs. You can also paint concrete with alkyd, latex, epoxy, or special floor paints. Some concrete floor paints contain a primer that can save you time by eliminating a step; talk to a paint specialist about the paint and primer that work best for you and your job.

1. Put on goggles and gloves. Follow the manufacturer's instructions to combine TSP (or TSP-PF) solution with water in a bucket. (Check out Chapter 2 for cleaning info.)

2. Mop the floor with the TSP solution, and let it dry thoroughly. Rinse out the mop and bucket with fresh water.

3. Wearing goggles and gloves, follow the manufacturer's instructions to combine etching acid with water in a bucket. Use a stir stick to mix the solution thoroughly. If you're going to paint the floor with alkyd paint, use muriatic acid (10 parts water to 1 part acid). For latex paint, use phosphoric acid (10 parts water to 1 part acid).

4. Pour a little etching solution on the concrete and, with the mop, spread the liquid uniformly in a small area. Repeat until you've etched the whole floor. Let it dry completely.

5. Use a vacuum to clean the etched concrete and remove dust and debris.

6. Use a stir stick to stir the primer (or combo primer/paint) thoroughly; pour ½ inch into roller tray reservoir.

7. With a 2½-inch tapered brush, cut in around the perimeter of the room.

8. Roll on primer in 4-foot sections with a 9-inch roller on an extension pole.

9. Continue rolling in the next 4-foot section until you complete the entire floor. Be sure not to paint yourself into a corner! Let the paint dry completely.

10. If the primer isn't a combo primer/paint, repeat Steps 6 through 9 with the desired concrete floor paint.

11. Let the floor paint dry thoroughly. You can walk on it as soon as it dries, but it's best to let it cure for a couple days before moving in furniture or rugs.

Some floor paints (epoxy, for one) look fabulous and hold up to wear but are slippery when painted on concrete, even when they're dry. Reduce the risk of slipping by adding nonslip silicate to the paint before you roll it on.

Color tricks for altering proportions

Interior designers use color to make a room's proportions seem perfect. Warm colors (like yellow, orange, and red) seem to come toward you. Cool colors (like green, blue, and violet) seem to move away. Use this basic color psychology to alter your room's proportions:

✔ To create intimacy on high ceilings, use deep, warm colors. Wood panels and beams are two increasingly popular solutions in large rooms.

✔ To create the impression of spaciousness and height, use light, cool colors, such as a tinted atmospheric blue for low ceilings.

✔ To make a squat, square room come alive, use faux tenting (painting alternating triangles of color that gather in the middle of the ceiling).

✔ To create instant coherence, tint your ceiling by painting it with a 25 percent tint of the wall color. Tinting the ceiling eliminates that chopped up look created by a big stark white expanse of ceiling.

✔ To tone down rooms with wallpapered or decidedly colored walls, use very pale blue, cream, peach, pink, or yellow for ceilings.

Chapter 9

Turning Your Brush to Trim, Windows, and Doors

Tasks performed in this chapter

- ✔ Painting trim, baseboards, and molding
- ✔ Painting double-hung windows
- ✔ Painting casement windows
- ✔ Painting paneled doors

Walls aren't the only surfaces that need painting. Baseboards, decorative moldings, and simple trims need a fresh coat of color not only to protect them from wear but also to complete your design statement. No matter what your room's style, you'll need to address your room's trim, molding, and baseboards.

Doors need painting for maintenance and decoration, too. A fresh coat of paint keeps them from warping and helps them look their best. Don't neglect the potential doors hold for adding style to rooms and hallways.

Windows often look worn sooner than doors and trim simply because temperature extremes on one side of the glass or the other cause condensation. It runs down the pane and collects on sills and mullions. If not wiped up, water eventually seeps under the paint and causes it to blister and peel; unprotected by paint, wood also soaks up moisture when it's raining, snowing, or just plain muggy outdoors. And nothing, not even nicked, scuffed doors, will make a freshly painted room look shabbier. You don't want to neglect the windows.

 If you're adding new trim to your room, your best bet is to prep and paint it before you apply it to the wall. The process is certainly easier and neater than painting it after it's already up — you don't have to worry about dripping and you don't have to be so careful around the edges. For more information on putting up trim, pick up a copy of *Home Improvement For Dummies* by Gene Hamilton and Katie Hamilton (Wiley).

Choosing the best finish for your trim, doors, and windows

Because trims, doors, and windows are often subject to lots of wear and tear, you may want a more durable and easy-to-clean finish. Alkyd or oil-based paints offer more protection against scuffing than latex or water-based paints and can be cleaned more easily. If you're using water-based, matte latex paint on walls, you may opt to use a semi-gloss or gloss version of the same color paint on trim. Semi-gloss finishes are far more durable than their matte counterparts and can stand up to a cleaning with mild detergent and a soft cloth to remove fingerprints and scuff marks.

Painting Trim, Baseboards, and Molding

Stuff You Need to Know

Toolbox:

- ✔ 2-inch blue painter's tape
- ✔ Trim shellac or sealer for previously stained wood (prevents bleeding)
- ✔ High-gloss finish latex trim paint
- ✔ Stir sticks
- ✔ 2-inch angled sash brush for wide trim
- ✔ Paint guard
- ✔ 1½-inch angled sash brush for narrow molding
- ✔ 1½-inch stubby-handled angled sash brush for tight spaces
- ✔ Clean rags
- ✔ Kneepads (optional)

Time Needed:
Less than half a day for one-coat painting

Trim is an umbrella term for any kind of finish strip applied around openings to conceal surface or angle joints and raw edges where drywall meets doorways, windows, floors, and ceilings. *Baseboards* are the finish strips between the floor and the wall and range in width from 3 to 18 inches. The term *molding* refers to larger and typically more ornamental finish strips. In this book, we use the term *trim* to apply to baseboards, moldings, and trim.

Getting any kind of trim to look perfectly smooth is no small feat. It requires a steady hand and good skills at maneuvering in tight spaces, often while kneeling (or lying) on the floor or extending your arm above your head.

Pick the right brush for the job. The principle is simple: small space, small brush. Try a tapered trim or sash brush. These brushes are small — from 1½ to 2 inches wide. Some have slant tips for sharp angles. Others have stubby handles for tight spaces. You may want to select two brushes — a smaller one for the sides of trim that project from the wall and a larger one for long runs of a wider, flatter surface that don't need to be as finely controlled.

It's easier to paint trim after painting the walls because you can control small tapered brushes a lot easier than you can control a roller. And if you tape adjoining walls with painter's tape, inadvertent brush marks stay on the tape, not on the wall. Even so, you'll find some painters who do just the reverse and swear by the results.

Before you start painting your trim, follow the same steps you would to prep your walls (see Chapters 2 and 3). Make sure you clean the trim thoroughly, fill all gaps and cracks, prep with a stain-blocker if necessary, and prime and sand to a smooth finish. If you're painting the entire room, the best time to prep trim is when you're prepping walls.

1. Use blue painter's tape to tape the edges of
the wall where they meet the edges of the
trim. (If you just taped and primed the trim,
you can skip this step.)

2. Stir the paint thoroughly with a stir stick,
and then dip a third of the bristles of your
2-inch angled sash brush into the paint can.
Tap both sides of the bristles on the can to
shake off extra paint, and then wipe the bristles against the side of the can to make sure
you get rid of excess paint. If you overload
the brush, you'll lose control of the paint
application.

Always work from the top down when you're painting trim, like professional painters do. If you don't have
ceiling molding, start at the top of a window or door frame. Always paint baseboards last. If you start at the
bottom, and then paint above, you risk bumping into wet paint or dislodging dust and debris that will stick to
the wet surface.

3. Position the paint guard at the bottom edge of the ceiling molding, at the top of the base-board, or on the wall adjacent to window and door frames. Hold the guard in your nondominant hand, using firm pressure to hold it in place.

4. Unload the paint with a stroke in one direction on the flattest, widest surface of the molding, trim, or baseboard. Press slightly — just enough to flex the bristles — and work slowly to ensure an even application of paint.

5. After you paint the first strip of wood, start subsequent strokes of the brush in a dry area, working toward the wet area. (This technique avoids creating lap marks.) Then raise the brush slightly and feather the edge. Feathering paint into a previously painted patch keeps the paint even and smooth from one stroke to another.

6. Reverse the direction of the brush, and lightly stroke back over the coat you just applied to set the paint.

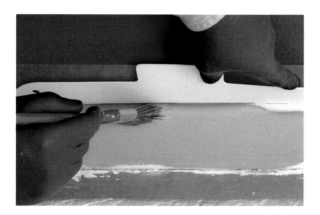

7. Use a 1½-inch angled sash brush to stroke the edges or underside of the trim, baseboard, or molding that juts out from the wall. In tight spaces, switch to using a stubby handled brush.

8. If you find that an area needs more paint, simply wait until the area is dry, sand lightly, and touch it up.

A paint guard prevents paint from winding up on surfaces. Still, keep clean rags on hand to clean up paint that may accidentally get on just-painted walls or other surfaces. For oil-based paints, speed up the cleanup with mineral spirits (paint thinner) — a little dab works wonders. For water-based paints, mix some mild detergent and water and dab up spatters with a clean cloth.

Jazzing up your room's molding

Does molding have to be white? No rule says that it has to be that way, but conventionally, trim is typically white. White trim can act as a thread to tie together different colored rooms because it keeps the eye moving through the space.

For the low ceilings in contemporary rooms, painting the trim the same color as the walls (or a shade or tint that's close) is usually best. This trick keeps the walls from being visually chopped up. Don't know how to decide? If you want your eye to travel to the trim or if your house needs a unifying thread, consider using white molding. Otherwise, match the color of your walls.

Painting Double-Hung Windows

Stuff You Need to Know

Toolbox:

- Screwdrivers
- 2-inch blue painter's tape
- 1½- or 2-inch angled sash brush (you get more precision with a smaller brush)
- Latex enamel or alkyd paint
- Paint guard
- 2½-inch angled sash brush
- Single-edge razor blade

Time Needed:

Less than half a day per window

The window frame (the part that encloses the glass and basic parts) may be made of wood, aluminum, or vinyl. Wood frames need painting for maintenance because water often condenses on the frame in winter and seeps under the paint, which can cause rot. In humid seasons, wood soaks up moisture, which can cause windows to warp, swell, or even shrink if neglected. Aluminum and vinyl are maintenance-free. That means you don't need to paint them to keep them functioning (that's always a good thing), but you may want to paint them to keep them looking beautiful.

Fix any damage to the windows before you get started. For tips, check out *Home Improvement For Dummies,* by Gene Hamilton and Katie Hamilton (Wiley).

1. Using appropriate screwdrivers, remove all the hardware — locks, curtain hooks, handles, and other metal devices — from the windows before you paint. Your painting job will go much faster and look much cleaner in the end.

2. Tape the glass all around the sash using 2-inch blue painter's tape.

3. If the upper, outer sash is movable, lower it to the bottom, leaving it open just an inch or two. Raise the lower, inner sash to midlevel. You're almost reversing their positions.

4. Rub an old candle or bar of soap over the wood jambs so that the windows will slide easily after you paint them. Make sure you don't paint the jambs themselves — that's what causes wood windows to stick. (If you have aluminum or vinyl windows, you can skip this step.)

TIP

If the upper sash won't move, it's probably been painted closed. Try hitting the wood on the sides where the window meets the jamb. Use no more than moderate force. Sometimes putting the tip of a screwdriver into the crack and then hitting the handle will break the paint seal. (Repeat placing the screwdriver in several different places along the jamb.) Just be careful! You don't want to hit and shatter the glass or go overboard hitting the frame with too much force. You don't want to add a trip to the emergency room to your paint project.

5. Dip no more than a third of the bristles of a narrow brush (1½- to 2-inch) into the paint can, tapping the brush, and then swiping each side against the can to remove excess paint.

6. Paint the lower part of the upper sash (remember that it's now in the low position). Paint the trim that's adjacent to the glass first, making certain that you paint right down to the glass, and then paint the wide horizontal board at the bottom.

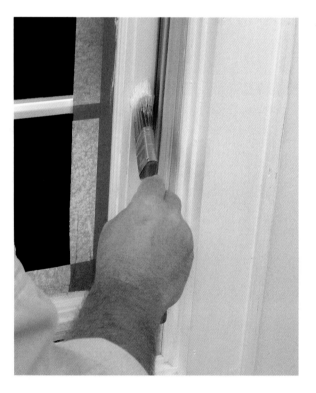

7. Paint the vertical sides of the upper, outer sash. If your window has mullions (slender, vertical bars that divide the windows), paint them last.

8. Raise the upper sash almost to the top and let it dry according to the paint manufacturer's instructions.

9. Move the inner sash down so that it's an inch or two from the bottom. Use your 1½- or 2-inch brush to paint the top edge of the inner sash — paint the flat, top edge first, and then the narrow trim, and finally the wide horizontal board.

10. Paint vertical boards of the inner sash with your 1½-inch brush, and then paint mullions if you have them.

11. Let the inner sash dry according to the paint manufacturer's instructions.

12. Using a paint guard to protect the wall and a 1½-inch tapered brush, paint the outside edges of the window frame.

13. Using a 2½-inch brush, paint the window frames, starting at the horizontal top portion and working down. Work from the inside toward the casing trim. Avoid painting any moving parts. Don't overload the brush with paint — you don't want it to seep into jambs.

14. Use a 2½-inch tapered brush to paint the window *sill* (also referred to as a *stool* — where the window rests against the wall) and *apron* (the trim on the wall below the sill). Let them dry.

15. Peel off tape, and/or use a single-edge razor blade to remove any paint drips on the glass as soon as possible.

16. Wait several hours for paint to dry before replacing locks and other hardware.

WARNING!

Paint windows early in the morning to allow for adequate drying time before you close them at night. You don't want wet paint drying your windows stuck.

TIP

When you're painting windows, you can create a moisture- and draft-proof seal between the glass and trim. Just lay the tape on the glass, leaving a straight, narrow edge of glass showing. Then as you work on an edge, also paint the glass. When you remove the tape, you end up with a weather-tight seal on the trim and glass.

Getting to know your windows

Windows aren't all created alike. Some windows crank open, others slide up and down, still others swing out, and some don't operate at all. *Double-hung windows* have an upper and lower sash (the inner frame that keeps the glass in place) that move up and down in their own individual channels. *Casement windows* have hinges on one side and open outward. *Awning windows* are hinged at the top and swing outward with the help of a lever or crank. *Hoppers,* the reverse of awnings, are hinged at the bottom and swing inward. *Jalousie windows* are composed of horizontal slats that are all connected and crank open at the same time.

Painting Casement Windows

Casement windows are a lot less complicated to paint than double-hung windows (see the previous project). You simply need to open them wide to reach all the areas. If your crank mechanism is broken or needs maintenance, fix it before painting to ensure that you don't accidentally mar the fresh paint later.

Semi-gloss and glossy paint are the best choices for window frames because they resist stains and are long wearing and easy to scrub. You can get them in water-based latex, which makes cleaning up afterward simple.

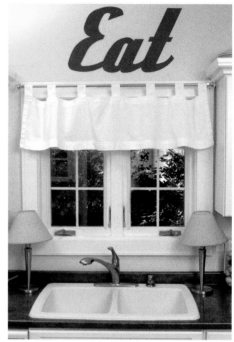

1. Using appropriate screwdrivers, remove all the hardware — locks, curtain hooks, handles, and other metal devices — from the windows before you paint. Your painting job will go much faster and look much cleaner in the end.

2. Decide whether you want to tape the window. You're going to paint the frame right down to the window to make a seal between the window and the frame. If you don't think you can paint a steady, thin line, tape the window first, leaving a hairline crack of glass visible between tape and frame. That will give you a neater "seal" than trying to do it freehand.

3. Crank the window open. Then load your 1½-inch tapered sash brush with paint by dipping the first third of the brush into the paint container. Tap the brush on the can, and wipe the sides of the brush against the can to remove excess paint.

4. Paint the narrow trim that meets the glass.

5. Paint horizontal surfaces of the window first, starting at the top and using a 2½-inch angled sash brush. Work from the inside edge of the open window toward the outer edge.

6. Paint vertical surfaces, working from the top to the bottom.

7. Paint the crossbars and frame casings with the 1½-inch tapered sash brush, doing horizontal surfaces first, top to bottom, and then vertical surfaces. You can get more precise control with the small brush if the crossbars and casings are narrow. Watch out for drips, and use the dry, clean, 2½-inch brush to wick up excess paint.

8. Use the 2½-inch angled sash brush to paint the window sill and apron.

9. If you taped the window in Step 1, take the tape off as soon as the paint dries. If you didn't tape the window, scrape off any dried paint spatters with a single-edged razor blade.

10. Let paint dry for 6 to 8 hours and then replace any hardware.

Painting Paneled Doors

Stuff You Need to Know

Toolbox:

- Screwdrivers
- Latex gloves
- Goggles
- TSP or TSP-PF
- Dropcloths
- Bucket
- Clean rags
- 180-grit sandpaper or electric finishing sander
- Liquid chemical deglosser (if you're covering semi-gloss or glossy paint)
- Primer
- 2½- or 3-inch angled sash brush
- Enamel or semi-gloss latex paint or alkyd paint
- Stir sticks
- 1½-inch angled sash brush
- Foam hot dog roller (optional; you can use the large brush instead)
- Pad painter (only if you don't remove the door)

Time Needed:

Less than half a day

Paneled doors are increasingly popular because of their appealing surface treatment. These traditional doors are a bit tricky to paint because they have multiple surfaces. Unlike their plain counterparts, paneled doors require a bit of patience and a more systematic approach to make them look their best.

For professional results, take down the door and remove all hardware. If you prefer to leave the door in place, cover the handle and all hardware with 2-inch blue painter's tape to avoid spatters.

Although this project describes painting a paneled door, you can follow Steps 1 through 9 plus 12 and 13 to paint a flat door. On paneled doors, start painting in the center and work your way to the flat outer edges. Before you begin, select a hot dog roller, or a 2½- or 3-inch brush to paint wide panels of the door.

1. Take the door off its hinges, using a screw-driver to push up on the pins. Get a helper to hold onto the door while you're working.

2. Lay the door flat on the floor (protected with a dropcloth), on sawhorses, or on chairs draped with dropcloths.

3. Using the appropriate screwdriver, remove doorknobs and other hardware.

4. Wearing gloves and goggles, mix a mild TSP or TSP-PF solution in a bucket, and use the solution and clean rags to remove dirt, grease, and oils from the door.

5. If the door is especially greasy, wipe on a degreaser and clean it with a rag. Let the door dry completely.

6. If the existing paint is chipped or the door has bumpy imperfections, go over the chips or imperfections with 180-grit sandpaper. Be sure to feather out the edges of the paint surrounding the chips. And wipe off dust with a clean damp rag.

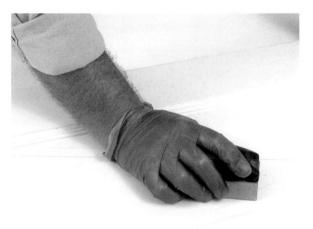

7. If the door has a hard, shiny finish or has been varnished, degloss the surface by wiping deglosser on with a clean rag until it feels tacky. You can let the deglosser dry if you just want to dull the surface so that you can repaint it with latex or glossy paint. But if you want to create a good bond for primer and paint, go to Step 8 about a half hour after you apply the deglosser. (In general, you should read the manufacturer's instructions for deglosser before you use it.)

8. Brush primer on the door, using a 2½-inch brush. Let it dry thoroughly. If you notice tiny imperfections in the primer that will show through on the finished layer, lightly sand the primer after it dries using 180-grit sandpaper.

9. Stir your paint thoroughly with a stir stick. Then start at the center of the door, using a 1½-inch tapered brush, and paint the trim on molded panels. Work from a corner and move out to the center of the trim to prevent excess paint from building up in corners.

10. Paint the flat surface of the raised or recessed panels, using a foam "hot dog" roller or a 2½- or 3-inch brush. Don't overload the brush or roller. Tap the brush on the sides of the paint can or roll the foam roller over the ridges in the paint tray to spread paint uniformly. (See Chapter 4 for more loading advice.)

11. Use your 2½- or 3-inch brush or hot dog roller to paint the flat edges of the door, using long continuous strokes. Apply paint to the horizontal outer and middle panels first, following the grain of the wood.

12. Paint the vertical panels of the door, again following the grain, and working from the top down to the bottom edge. To keep surfaces smooth, paint from dry areas stroking toward wet paint.

13. Let the paint dry and cure according to the paint manufacturer's instructions before remounting hardware and hanging the door. If you didn't take down the door, try to keep it ajar for as long as possible after you paint it. Although paint dries to the touch in 24 hours, it can take as long as a week for it to cure. The longer you can wait, the less you risk the surface becoming marred.

If you're interested in painting each face of the door a different color, you may not be sure what color to paint the edges of the door. The rule of thumb is to paint the edges to match the face that's visible when you open the door. If a door swings into a blue room from a yellow hall, paint the edges yellow — the same color as the hall door face.

Check the bottom edge of the door to see whether it has been finished. A finished edge prevents the wood from absorbing moisture and warping. If it hasn't been sealed, sand it to remove imperfections, and then prime the unfinished edge. (If you didn't remove the door from its hinges, slip an unframed mirror under it to see whether it's finished. If not, use a pad painter to prime it.)

Part IV
The Part of Tens

The 5th Wave   By Rich Tennant

"Oh, Philip, I don't know why you insist on doing this yourself, but if you get so much as a drop of paint on the crown jewels, I shall be furious."

In this part . . .

If you're looking for sage advice on choosing colors or improving your paint job, you've come to the right place. We don't bog you down with details in this part — we get straight to the point, giving you ten quick tips to help you in your quest to make the most of your painting projects.

Chapter 10

Ten Tips for a Practically Perfect Paint Job

he ten tips in this chapter help you get it right the first time. Keep reading if you want to unlock the secrets to practically perfect paint.

Start with a Clean Surface

Giving dingy walls a fresh coat of paint spruces up your living space. But if you paint over dust, grime, and other dirt, you won't like the result. Wash your walls with a mixture of trisodium phosphate (TSP) and water before you paint.

Take the Time to Tape

We know that when you buy that bright new color, the only thing you want to do is start painting. Taking the time to tape may seem like an irritating delay, but it's essential. Put blue painter's tape around anything you want to protect from paint, including baseboards, ceilings, window and door frames, and electrical switches.

Use Primer

If you cleaned, but your walls are stained, or if you're painting your walls a lighter color than they were before, primer is a must. It seals stains and gives you a clean, even surface on which to paint. Imperfections can adhere to wet primer, and sometimes particles are found in the primer itself. That's why professional painters sand a primed surface after it dries. But if you don't mind a few minor imperfections, you can skip sanding and start painting after the primer dries.

Go Stir Crazy

Paint settles fast. Keep lots of stir sticks handy and stir frequently. Every time your paint container needs to be refilled, stir the paint in the can. A good 30 to 60 seconds of stirring keeps your paint color uniform.

Use the Best Tools You Can Afford

You don't have to spend a fortune to get quality painting tools, but you want to buy the best you can afford. Painting is easier when you're using quality brushes and roller covers — and you don't have to worry about bristles falling out and sticking to the wall. Quality materials also help you achieve better results; sometimes a sloppy paint job has nothing to do with the painter and everything to do with the tools.

Don't Pinch Pennies on Paint

You see an oh-so-beautiful swatch of pricey paint. You take the chip to the home improvement store to have it analyzed so you can buy the "same" color in a cheaper paint. Good idea to save money? Not exactly. You won't get the same color or finish in a cheaper product. Pricey paints have more pigments and greater complexity of pigments to create the color. That's why they cost more.

Invest in a Power Roller

If you have lots of painting to do, invest in a power roller, which promises fast painting, uniform coverage, no dripping, no paint trays, no stirring, no reloading, no spattering, and easy cleanup. It's also portable. Prices range from $40 to $200.

Use a Power Sprayer

Power paint sprayers make covering large surfaces easy, especially on irregular or complicated surfaces, such as louvered doors, panels, and trim. Some relatively inexpensive consumer models are available. Read the manufacturer's directions about adjusting your paint's viscosity (thickness) so that it can be sprayed. Some do-it-yourselfers find that high-volume, low-pressure (HVLP) sprayers work better than consumer sprayers. HVLPs are more costly than some consumer sprayers, but many painters swear that they end up with less overspray, better coverage, and a finer finish.

Be Detail-Oriented

In a newly painted room, details that make the most difference are the things that most painters seem to miss while they're painting — think air registers or air ducts, radiators, closet doors . . . the things that tend to stick out like sore thumbs when you're finished. Make these eyesores fade into the background by painting them using surface-friendly paint tinted to match or complement your wall color.

Give Your Paint Plenty of Time to Dry

You've done everything right up 'til now. Don't waste your effort by putting furniture — or children or pets — back in the room too early. Be patient while your paint dries; you'll have plenty of time to enjoy the results afterward!

Chapter 11

Ten Tips for Picking the Best Color

ou don't have to hire a decorator to turn your home into a haven. Find the colors that achieve what you want by using these pro tips for choosing colors.

Spin the Color Wheel

Being familiar with the standard color wheel can help you pick the best paint and decorations for your home. Go to `www.artsparx.com/colorwheel.asp` to see how primary colors, secondary colors, and tertiary colors work together.

Assess Intensity and Value

How pure, bright, or dull a color is refers to its *intensity*. Think of fire engine red and bright mustard yellow as high intensity colors. Sky blue and beige are low intensity colors. Every color, no matter its intensity, has a range of *values* from light to dark. Paint chips show a color, such as blue, and five to seven hues ranging from lightest to darkest in intensity and value. Use one to assess how the color will look on your wall. The safest selection is usually one of the two colors in the middle of the strip.

Know Your Color Scheme

The three categories to keep in mind as you evaluate colors for your room are complementary, analogous, and neutrals. Complementary décor combines a primary and secondary color found opposite each other on the color wheel (example: red and green). Analogous colors fall into two groups: warm (shades of red, orange, and yellow) and cool (colors in the green, blue, and violet range). Neutrals are browns, beiges, taupes, whites, and blacks not included on a color wheel; they're considered non-colors.

Visualize the Undertones in Colors

Sometimes perceptions of a color change dramatically, depending on what's next to it. All colors, other than the three primaries, are mixed colors. So you can't just assume, for example, that a can of white paint will go with everything in your home; it may take on pink undertones when you see it next to a red Oriental rug. Most people don't see undertones until it's too late. Fortunately, you can rely on clerks at the paint store. Take a focal piece (like a pillow sham, carpet sample, or photo if your item is too big) to give the clerk what he needs to help you avoid problems with undertones.

Evaluate Natural and Artificial Light

Before selecting paint, consider lighting. Look at paint chips under direct, indirect, and artificial light. Evaluate the samples against furniture and rugs. After you narrow your choices, get a small jar of each finalist and brush each on a piece of white poster board. After the paint dries, tape the poster board to the wall and evaluate again. Assessing larger color samples ensures that you're making the right choice for your room.

Create a Mood with Color

Color affects mood and the way you perceive the comfort level of a space. For a calm effect, select cool colors. To energize your home, look to the warm color palette. Pair a warm color with a cooler complement to create energy.

Change a Room's Size with Color

Warm colors advance and cool colors recede. If you want to make a small room appear larger, paint it a pale, cool, less intense color. If you have a large room that needs downsizing, use warm colors or darker, more intense hues.

Consider Colors in Adjacent Rooms

You don't have to use the same color scheme in adjoining rooms, but you have a more peaceful ambiance if one room naturally flows into the next. Select complementary color schemes, or vary the intensity of one hue, going from the lightest shade to the most dramatic. Don't create a hodge podge of loud, conflicting colors — if each room is competing, you won't be able to relax.

Coordinate with Furniture and Flooring

Using a favorite painting or rug to inspire a color scheme highlights that piece when the room is done. The trick is to choose a paint color that blends with the piece instead of matching it exactly. Paint stores have cards that show coordinated colors; you see a decorated room, chips of dominant paint, and colors that go with them.

Play It Safe with Neutrals

Neutrals blend in, are flexible, and cooperate with other colors. White is especially good at opening spaces. Warm neutrals work well in rooms with few or small windows. Black is a great accent, but use it sparingly. Neutrals are considered "safe" wall treatments. If you're selling your home, neutrals are the way to go. Most potential buyers can visualize their furnishings set before those freshly painted walls.

Index